Made in United States
Orlando, FL
09 March 2025

powerful Zionistic and social action, with a curious soul, fresh as a child's. You had a rare equilibrium, you were balanced, independent and these qualities gave you a comfortable and charming and magnetic pleasantness."

Professor Mimi Eisenstadt, Dean of the School of Social Work at the Hebrew University, described Eliezer in her eulogy as someone who had always had one foot in academia and a second foot in practice and as a social entrepreneur he was ahead of his time. "A man of immense integrity, a man of nobility of spirit and vision, a humble and caring man, sensitive and pleasant-mannered. But perhaps most of all, many of the faculty at our school will remember you as their mentor, as the one who accompanied them throughout their academic careers, as a source of knowledge and as one who always gave support and a good word at the right time, with wise advice and a lot of encouragement. For us, Eliezer Jaffe is a model of the person who is a social worker." Ofir Ozeri and Sagi Balasha parted from Eliezer on behalf of Ogen. Balasha promised to continue to cause Eliezer's vision to blossom and grow. "Your glorious legacy will always be a candle to our feet, especially at this time, as we develop the organization in new directions. We will continue on your path and we will see to it that in the future there will be hundreds of thousands of families who will be saved thanks to the great enterprise you began."

Almost all the eulogizers quoted in their words Eliezer's beautiful statement which he repeated on many occasions: "Life is a loan that one day we will have to repay with interest, and the interest is to make the world a little better than the one we entered."

Eliezer Jaffe returned his soul to his Creator with a huge interest in good deeds.

**A Social Pioneer**
Elyashiv Reichner
Eliezer D. Jaffe

Producer & International Distributor
eBookPro Publishing
www.ebook-pro.com

**A Social Pioneer**
**Elyashiv Reichner and Eliezer D. Jaffe**

Copyright © 2022 Elyashiv Reichner and Eliezer D. Jaffe

All rights reserved; No parts of this book may be reproduced or transmitted in any form or by any means, electronic or mechanical, including photocopying, recording, taping, or by any information retrieval system, without the permission, in writing, of the author.

Translation and footnotes: Toby Klein Greenwald
Copyediting by Leiah Jaffe

Contact: naomieini1@gmail.com
ISBN 9798376619056

# A SOCIAL PIONEER

**ELYASHIV REICHNER
ELIEZER D. JAFFE**

TRANSLATED BY
TOBY KLEIN GREENWALD

# Contents

| | |
|---|---|
| Introduction: All Have Gathered Here | 7 |
| Translator's Note | 11 |
| Chapter One: A New Immigrant | 13 |
| Chapter Two: An Israeli Family | 29 |
| Chapter Three: Enlisting Without Being Called Up | 39 |
| Chapter Four: From University to the Jerusalem Municipality | 50 |
| Chapter Five: Blessed with Children | 69 |
| Chapter Six: A Family Man | 87 |
| Chapter Seven: "The One You Have Loved, Yitzhak" | 99 |
| Chapter Eight: Giving an Equal Opportunity | 114 |
| Chapter Nine: The Rights of the Neighborhoods | 116 |
| Chapter Ten: For the Good of the Child | 130 |
| Chapter Eleven: Giving Wisely | 146 |
| Chapter Twelve: Partnership Philanthropy | 158 |
| Chapter Thirteen: The Israel Free Loan Association - "Ogen" | 169 |
| Chapter Fourteen: Looking to the Future | 189 |
| Chapter Fifteen: Farewell | 209 |

*This book is dedicated to those who wish to improve the world through social involvement.*

# Introduction

## All Have Gathered Here

**A note from Elyashiv Reichner, author of the Hebrew edition**

On the eve of Rosh Chodesh Sivan 2019, a memorial service was held at the Yad Sarah building in Jerusalem to mark the anniversary of the death of Professor Eliezer David Jaffe. Anyone who did not get to know Eliezer in his lifetime would have been introduced that evening to the size of his personality and to his many works. In addition to his children, grandchildren, and the rest of his family, present at the event were many members of the Israel Free Loan Association (IFLA), the association he founded in 1990 in a small apartment in Jerusalem, that over the years became the largest organization in the world providing interest-free loans.

Also present were people who knew Eliezer from his many years of activity for Zahavi, an organization that worked to promote the status of families blessed with many children. There were also members of non-profits and third-sector organizations, who had the privilege of receiving priceless tips from Eliezer, as he was a great expert in philanthropy. This included information on how to run an association, how to raise funds for it and how to expand its activities. Additionally, there were academics, students from the forty years

of Eliezer's teaching at the School of Social Work at the Hebrew University, who became colleagues and friends.

However, even the diverse group gathered in the Jerusalem hall could not fully reflect Eliezer's multifaceted personality. The hall has not yet been built that could accommodate the many people Eliezer helped in his lifetime. Many of them are not even aware of his direct and indirect impact on their lives.

Eliezer's official title was misleading. He was a professor of social work, one of the founders and teachers of the first social work schools in the country, who left an indelible mark on the profession through his many studies and books. No less, he was also a social pioneer who never isolated himself in the academic ivory tower, but was always present in the field of social action and led many actions that were significant and he brought to his social action the knowledge he acquired through research.

As director of the Jerusalem Municipal Department of Family and Community Services in the early 1970s, he reshaped the nature of the social worker's tasks in the city, and was fortunate to see how some of the new patterns he established were later adopted by all authorities throughout the country.

As head of the admissions committee of the School of Social Work at the Hebrew University, he opened the gates of academia to students who had not been given an equal opportunity in the educational system in which they studied. As a researcher of the restoration of the Yemin Moshe neighborhood in Jerusalem, he left a significant mark on neighborhood restoration projects throughout the country. As a researcher in the field of child welfare, he contributed to the legal regulation of the adoption of children from foreign countries. As the founder of the "Giving Wisely" website and by assisting in bringing the GuideStar website to Israel, he made a crucial

contribution to transparency in the world of *amutot* (charitable associations) and non-profit organizations. He was a man of vision and of action (in Hebrew: *na'eh doresh v'naeh mekayem*).[1]

However, even Eliezer Jaffe's many studies and activities do not tell the full story of the man. The story of Eliezer Jaffe is also the story of a new immigrant, who came on his own from the United States to the young State of Israel, leaving behind parents and siblings, and who later served as the bridgehead for the absorption of their descendants in Israel. This is the story of a Zionist social activist who, from his first encounter with Israeli society, did not stop asking himself how he could contribute to society, to the absorption of the many immigrants who joined it, and to reducing the social gaps within it. This is the story of an honest and humble man, who loved the country, and a beloved man, who, in addition to all his activities for the good of society, succeeded in fulfilling his dream of creating in Israel, together with his beloved wife Rivka, a large Israeli family, all of them involved in activities that benefit Israeli society.

I was happy to get to know the late Eliezer Jaffe while he was still alive. His wife Rivka, of blessed memory, was the sister of my Savta (Grandma) Leah, she should have a long life. When I eagerly read the book "Letters to Yitz," in which Eliezer gathered the correspondence between himself and his older brother Yitzhak Yonah (Yitz), I was exposed to his Zionist roots and his social perceptions. In an interview I conducted with him for the Makor Rishon newspaper, I was fortunate to be exposed to the important studies he conducted and to his other activities, but only with the writing of this book did I have the privilege of getting to know, on a deeper level, his impressive personality and the extent of his contribution to Israeli society.

---

1   One of the sources for this is the Talmud Bavli, Hagiga, 14:b.

It is my privilege to thank all those who helped in writing this book. First of all, I am grateful to the four children of the late Eliezer and Rivka - Uri, Yael, Naomi and Ruti -- for allowing me to write the chapters of their father's life. Thank you also to his children's spouses – Keren, Moshe, Ohad and Udi -- and to their children -- Eliezer's grandchildren -- and to all the other members of the extended family who assisted in the work. Thank you to the family of the Israel Free Loan Association, now known as "Ogen" ("Anchor"), which continues Eliezer's path, and to all the many other interviewees who devoted their time to help in gathering materials and for sharing their many stories about Eliezer.

## Translator's Note

Translating Elyashiv Reichner's book on Eliezer Jaffe, of blessed memory, began as a labor of love and evolved into a journey of discovery. Even though I grew up in Cleveland, praying in the same synagogue as the Jaffe family, knew some of the children of the Jaffe "tribe" from our Bnei Akiva youth group, and have lived in Israel since 1967, where Eliezer became well known for his important work, I was astonished to discover the extent to which so many of Eliezer's actions have affected the lives of those of us privileged to live in the Holy Land. Stories about his family roots and the behavior of his parents and the wider family provide us with additional role models and add to the tapestry of his rich and exemplary life.

I have added footnotes to clarify and simplify some cultural and historical references that would be familiar to most Hebrew readers, but not necessarily to English readers, especially those who live outside of Israel.

The first time a Hebrew word is used, it is italicized and explained, and after that it is not, for easier reading. I have usually transliterated the "chet/het" using an "h" except for in the case of proper names and a few other exceptions.

My heartfelt thanks to Naomi Jaffe Eini, Eliezer's daughter, with whom I consulted extensively. Thank you also to Ruth Lieberman Jaffe and Elyashiv Reichner, MSN, JD, RN, who were generous with

their time. Thank you to Arnie Draiman who answered questions regarding non-profit terminology. Additional people with whom I consulted regarding certain words or phrases in the areas of education, academia, law, ethnicity and medicine were Dr. Yael Barenholtz, Professor Jeffrey Woolf, Adv., Tamar Rubin, Itay Peretz, Rabbi Avraham Bensoussan, Henya Storch, M.S.N., and Fruma Farkas Aspir, J.D., R.N. Having said that, any errors are my own.

When I sent the final chapter to Naomi, she asked me, "How did you feel when you wrote the end?" to which I replied, "I cried."

I hope that you, the reader, will also be moved by this book, and that Eliezer's story will serve as an inspiration to us all to be better people and to do what we can to improve the world in which we live.

Toby Klein Greenwald
Elul, 5781
August, 2021

# Chapter One

## A New Immigrant

In September, 1960, Elul Elul 5720, Eliezer David Jaffe, a 27-year-old American Jew, disembarks from a ship at the port of Haifa. He is making aliya to Israel, on his own, from the city of Cleveland, Ohio in the USA. He is making aliya because he is a Zionist, leaving behind, across the ocean, his parents, four brothers and many friends.

Eliezer arrived in Israel as a social pioneer out of a desire to contribute to the creation of social services in the young country, founded only twelve years earlier. He was making aliya to Jerusalem, as a young Ph.D. of Social Work, in order to become integrated into the first university faculty of social work in Israel.

After a number of weeks, during which he was hosted by relatives on his mother's side in Haifa, Eliezer went up to Jerusalem and settled into a new immigrant apartment block. He moved from a large home in Cleveland, with three floors, and front and back yards, to a tiny one-room apartment. He knew very little Hebrew. He was told that his first year at the Hebrew University he could teach in English, but he wanted to wait until he acquired the language, and insisted on teaching his students in Hebrew, though with a strong American accent.

Eliezer's children relate that he told them that during the same time period there were students who asked him to teach in his mother tongue, due to the difficulty in understanding him when he taught in "the father tongue" (Hebrew), but he persevered. The first three days of the week Eliezer studied Hebrew in an ulpan for new immigrants together with people from various places in the diaspora.

From the first moment, he wanted to be an Israeli, and he didn't look for friends among other new immigrants from America, who in any case were very few in those years. Thus, at the age of 27, Eliezer found himself living alone in the capital city of Israel without a wife and without a family, without knowing the local language and without a community, but totally at peace with the Zionist decision he had made.

Eliezer's path could have been totally different. He could have expressed the great love he had for Israel, that he had imbibed in his parents' home and in the Hashomer Hadati (Hebrew for "The Religious Guard") organization, in other ways, as his parents, brothers and many friends had done, but who remained in America. However, Eliezer was imbued with Zionism and from childhood he identified strongly with the segments in prayers where "Eretz Yisrael" and "going up to Eretz Yisrael" were mentioned. Many Holocaust survivors who arrived in America after WWII reinforced his feeling that the place of the Jews was only in the land of Israel, and when he grew up, he was determined to raise his children there. Twice he was close to marrying nice young Jewish women who he knew in Cleveland, but he chose to cut off contact with them because they refused to move to Israel.

When Eliezer was thirteen, his brother Yitzhak (Yitz), at 20-years-old, left their parents' home, and against their wishes joined an

agricultural farm of Hashomer Hadati in New Jersey. Hashomer Hadati was the Zionist youth group that had been active in Europe during WWII and had branched out to North America. It combined Zionist pioneering activities with adherence to mitzvot (commandments) and the Jewish tradition.

Together with many other friends, Yitz received training at the agricultural farm for life on kibbutz, with the goal to make aliya to Israel and join one of the religious kibbutzim. At a certain stage, Yitz was appointed head of the training program and invited Eliezer and their younger brother, Jack, to join him. It was a good opportunity for the younger brothers to taste a bit of the Zionist pioneering spirit that had captured the heart of their older brother.

The State of Israel was established in 1948 and Yitz already had an aliya date, planning to make aliya in the autumn of 1949. Everyone already knew that Yitz was on his way to Israel, but then things changed. It was in the summer of 1949, a few weeks before his date of aliya, during a visit at the Hashomer Hadati branch in Brooklyn, New York, that Yitz met Miriam, who was a *madricha* (counselor) at that branch and they became friends. Throughout the summer their connection deepened, and it caused a change in Yitz's plans to move to Israel.

Miriam was already a social work student at Columbia University and she did not see herself stopping her studies to make aliya to Israel to live on a young and challenging kibbutz. Her dedication to her students, and Yitz's dedication to the family business headed by his father, caused Yitz to postpone his aliya. He stayed in America, built a family with Miriam, and began to work in his father's company. Yitz stayed a great Zionist his whole life, as the story will yet be told, but at that stage he froze his plans to move to Israel.

Eliezer, who had been deeply impacted by the Zionist aspirations

of his older brother, decided to create his own path in life. He made it clear to his parents, over and over again, that he was determined to make aliya.

The first time Eliezer visited Israel was in 1957, three years before his aliya. He arrived in Israel in response to a request the Jewish Agency had made to various American professionals -- to come and volunteer for a specific time period. Eliezer responded to the call and came to volunteer as a social worker in the Talpiot *ma'abara*[2] in southern Jerusalem. There were close to ten thousand new immigrants living in the ma'abara, who had been part of the great wave of aliya after the establishment of the state.

Eliezer worked for those who headed the Department of Public Health of Hadassah Hospital, who were working to stem the tide of illnesses that were rampant as a result of the difficult life in the ma'abara.

In the meager tents and huts of the ma'abara, Eliezer the American, who was of European descent, met Jews from Morocco, Iraq, Persian and Kurdistan for the first time in his life. He was exposed to the cultural and language diversity that the great ingathering of the exiles to the state had brought with it. The winter months in the ma'abara were especially harsh, and people had to cope not only with the weather, but with the heavy poverty that existed there. Eliezer suddenly met the human face of all the theories that he had learned about in his Psychology and Sociology studies.

The unmediated meeting with the hardships of the new olim shattered, for Eliezer, the utopian dream of an ideal country, flowing with milk and honey, but it did not fracture in the least his love of

---

2   *ma'abara*- low quality "hut" housing for new immigrants, mostly from Northern Africa and other Arab countries.

Israel, and did not deter his desire to make aliya and to settle in the land. Just as he was to behave throughout his life, the social challenges that he encountered did not deter him; on the contrary. They inspired him to work, to identify the needs, and to find solutions.

The period of his volunteering in the Jerusalem ma'abara clarified for Eliezer the urgency of the problems to be solved. He was exposed to the challenge of absorption, unprecedented in the young country still only nine years old. A country with only 600,00 people at the time of its establishment, absorbed in its first decade close to a million *olim* (new immigrants).

Eliezer wanted to take part in this great challenge. He identified the urgent need the young state had of social workers with an academic education who would know how to cope with the many social challenges that came together with the mass aliya. Eliezer did not settle for fulfilling his personal desire to be a field social worker. He aspired to contribute to the formulation of social policy in the young state and, to this end, he knew he had to acquire professional knowledge and to progress in the academic world. He formed a plan in his heart -- to complete his doctoral studies in social work in America, and only then to make aliya. Then he would join in the absorption of olim and in designing the face of the Israeli welfare system.

Eliezer wasn't the only one in his family who came to Israel for a short volunteering period. A short time before his arrival, his brother Alvin came for similar reasons. Alvin was an engineer, and, like Eliezer, he identified many challenges that the young country had during that time period. He came to Israel for six months, and then returned to America where he established his family.

About a year after Eliezer went back to Cleveland to complete his studies, the first academic school for social work was founded in Israel. Something that precipitated the creation of this school, as

was recorded eventually in the biography of Dr. Israel Katz, one of its first directors, was a scathing report about the social services in Israel that was written in 1957 by Professor Philip Klein of Columbia University. The report strongly criticized the welfare policy in Israel and pointed to a list of societal failures. Among them, claimed Professor Klein in his report, was the fact that the training of social workers in Israel was not carried out at the level and in the numbers that the state required.

Even before Klein penned his report, it was known in the Joint (an American Jewish charitable organization), that there was a necessity for the creation of an academic school for social workers in Israel. The number of academically trained social workers in the first decade of the state was miniscule and amounted to less than a minyan. The number of social work doctoral candidates could be counted on one hand.

And yet, not everyone excitedly adopted the idea of an academic school of social work. In spite of the fact that in America it was already clear during the same era, that the profession of social work must be an academic profession learned in university, there were those who opposed it in young Israeli academia. This was mostly out of a lack of respect for the profession and because of a perception that people needed to help themselves, and that there was no reason to create an academic profession to help people.

In the end, in response to pressure from the Joint, the School of Social Work was opened in Jerusalem in 1958, formed by a partnership between the Ministry of Welfare and Hebrew University. The first director of the school was Dr. Eileen Blakey of America, who after WWII traveled around Europe and photographed Jewish children. Blakey designed the syllabus according to the American perception that she was familiar with, and, naturally, she looked for

an academic faculty who believed in the same approach.

She began by looking for people in American universities, and turned, among others, to the university in Cleveland where Eliezer was studying. Dr. Blakey looked for a person who would move to Israel in order to establish a research division in the new school and she offered the position to Eliezer, and Eliezer hastened to accept the opportunity.

However, he was not encouraged by his family and by the community in Cleveland. Many of them found it difficult to understand why an older, single man, who just completed his Ph.D. and was about to embark on his career, would choose to leave his parents and his family and make aliya to the young and unsafe State of Israel. His parents, even though they were Zionists, tried to talk Eliezer out of his decision to make aliya. They even tried to "bribe" him with a promise to buy him a home in their neighborhood, but nothing could change his mind. He was determined to take on the pioneering challenge that had been brought to his door. Two months after completing his doctorate, he made aliya and joined the academic faculty of the young university school.

If we fast forward a bit, we will discover that less than a year after his aliya, Eliezer, the new immigrant, already stood under the *huppa* (wedding canopy) in Jerusalem, where he married Rivka. At the age of 28 he was fortunate to fulfill more than a few of his dreams. He established a home with an Israeli woman in Eretz Yisrael, taught in Hebrew at an Israeli university, and trained social workers for the welfare system of the young country that he loved. But his dreams didn't stop with that. Eliezer was only at the beginning of his personal, family, professional and civic journey, and many adventures awaited him. But first, it's significant to get to know the home in which he grew up, his roots, and the values on which he was raised.

Henry (Elhanan) Jaffe and Sarah Zipperstein, Eliezer's parents, immigrated in their youth from Europe to America before WWI, as many Jews did in that time period. Henry was born in the village Širvintosin southeast Lithuania and Sarah was born in the city Kovel', that was then in Russia, today in the Ukraine. They arrived in Cleveland, the county seat of Cuyahoga County, which was the largest region in the state of Ohio. They met each other in a social framework where young Jews got together, married and raised a family.

In his introduction to the book "Letters to Yitz" Eliezer writes, "Like thousands of other immigrant Jewish families who came to forge new lives in the *Goldene Medina* (Yiddish for "The Golden State"), our parents struggled hard to survive in their new surroundings, not only economically, but also – especially – as Jews. 'Being Jewish' meant having five children, a Zionist orientation to events in Palestine, a modern Orthodox household with observance of traditional religious practices, and above all, a Jewish education for the children."

*Shul* (synagogue) and *Shabbat* (the Sabbath) were central in the life of the Jaffe family. Henry Jaffe was the vice president of the largest Orthodox shul in Cleveland (Taylor Road Synagogue), in which thousands of families were members. He was also one of the *hazanim* (cantors) on holidays and the High Holidays. He made a livelihood from his paper and material recycling shop and he used to sing cantorial selections to himself as he would wrap packages or while driving his truck to collect merchandise.

Sarah Jaffe was a housewife, and since Henry was busy in the shop till late at night, she was the main educator of the children, and responsible for the discipline in the home. Eliezer writes that his mother was steadfast in her decision that her children will succeed

in America, and she saw to it that every day they received four hours of Jewish studies and Hebrew in a Talmud Torah at the end of their public school day.

The Jaffe home in Cleveland, during Eliezer's childhood years, was not a large home. There were three rooms with one bathroom, but this fact did not prevent it from being a home that was open to many guests. When guests were there – Jack the youngest brother recalls -- the four sons would crowd together in one bed and sleep "heads and tails." Sometimes they also slept on the floor. Eliezer attributed his mother's attribute of welcoming guests to her memories of the days when she was a young immigrant in America and was in need of the kindness of others. Sarah left her parents' home at the age of only 14 and she wrote to her father later how she saved every ruble that he had put into her little hands at the train station before she set out on her journey. To her sorrow, she never saw him again.

Sarah began to work as a seamstress in order to support herself, and she was fortunate to be unofficially adopted by a warm and caring Jewish family. These memories influenced her when the local child services in Cleveland put out a call to Jewish families to accept children who were saved in the Holocaust, as foster children. She brought home two siblings and raised them to adulthood and financial independence, just as she did with her five biological children. This actually had a great influence on her son Eliezer, who became a researcher and promoted the topic of fostering and adoption among children in Israel.

In addition to *hachnasat orhim*, hosting guests, the Jaffe family was a home of *tzedaka*, charity. Yocheved Levi relates how when she and her husband Yossi were *shlihim* in Cleveland (emissaries), they lived for a period of time in the Jaffe home. She relates that there was a large bowl on the family dining table in the living room, with

dollar bills in it, intended for the many people who came to the home requesting tzedaka. Sarah instituted a motto, that was, "Anyone who knocks on our door will not leave empty-handed."

The Jaffe home was a central station for shlihim who arrived from Eretz Yisrael, especially those from the Zionist organizations Hashomer Hadati and Bnei Akiva. More than once Eliezer would talk about the mornings that he would wake up and find unknown guests in his room who had arrived at the family home late at night and found a warm bed there. At some point the Jaffe family put out a guest book in which their many guests could write their impressions of their visits in the Cleveland Jewish community and of their warm hosting in the Jaffe home.

In his book "Letters to Yitz" Eliezer wrote, "Mom's religious upbringing was fundamentalist. She had a personal 'contract' with G-d: she would raise her children as believing, committed Jews, keep a Jewish home and be genuinely charitable, and G-d, for his part, would watch over the family. The arrangement worked fairly well, even when her brother Alex (Shaiya, or Yehoshua, in Hebrew) and her sister Dora (Devorah) were killed in a tragic head-on automobile accident which left Mom and Pa miraculously untouched in the death car. Over the years, when things were difficult, Mom would go to sit near Alex and Dora's graves at the Lansing Road Jewish cemetery and ask them to intervene with G-d for the family, for the children, for the Jews."

The five children born to Henry and Sarah Jaffe were Alice, the oldest, and then came the four sons: Arthur, in Hebrew "Yitzhak," in short, "Yitz"; Alvin, in Hebrew "Avraham," Lester, in Hebrew "Eliezer" and then Jack, in Hebrew "Yaakov." Eliezer was born on the tenth day of Kislev, 5694, November 28, 1933. His years of study in elementary school began during WWII, during the terrible Shoah that took place in Europe.

The Jews in Cleveland encountered almost no anti-Semitism but the children of the Jaffe family suffered occasionally from the catcalls of Gentile children, on their way to school and one day the Jaffe children decided to react. It was after some boys shouted at them, "Wait till WWII is over and then we'll hurt the Jews." Eliezer and his brothers waited for the opportunity and they pounced on one of the boys who was harassing them, and after that the catcalls stopped.

The central difficulty they had, living as Jewish children in Cleveland, did not stem from manifestations of anti-Semitism, which were few, but from the distance that was created between the Jewish children and the Gentile children, mainly for halachic reasons. Eliezer and his brothers could not be hosted at or eat at the homes of their classmates who were not Jewish, and these limitations forced upon them a distance and a certain isolation from their social environment.

As young men, the four sons worked every summer in their father's shop in order to be near him, and they were privileged to imbibe from him the values of hard work. Yitz, the oldest, spent more time in the shop than his younger brothers. He inherited from his father the desire to work hard and, as the oldest brother, from among the boys, he felt a great responsibility to help his father. Eliezer also worked in the shop, but as a spindly boy who had suffered since childhood from back problems, he was less capable than his brothers of physical labor.

There were seven years between Yitz and Eliezer. Eliezer saw in Yitz not only an older brother, but also a role model to emulate. As a little boy he would see Yitz active in founding the local religious Zionist youth movement, Hashomer Hadati, and turn it into one of the biggest and most active branches in the country. He was impressed by the Zionist fervor of his brother and by his plan to make

aliya to Israel. Many of those who visited the Jaffe home were friends of Yitz from the movement and they aroused in the young Eliezer the desire to understand why people have such a yearning to go to Israel. When Yitz left home and went on *Hachshara* (Hebrew for a preparatory program meaning "Preparation") of Hashomer Hadati in New Jersey, Eliezer, who was thirteen-years-old, felt a strong sense of the parting. He was convinced that his big brother was about to move to Israel.

Toby Klein Greenwald, who grew up in the same community as the Jaffe family in Cleveland, remembers father Henry and the four sons sitting next to each other in one row in their shul. She remembers Henry as being very involved in the lives of the young people in the community, and his sons, following his example, also became leaders in the community. She describes the children of the Jaffe family as torches who lit the way and inspired the members of the community.

Inspired by Yitz, the younger brothers – Eliezer, Alvin and Jack – were active in the branch of Hashomer Hadati in Cleveland. Eliezer even served for a while as the branch chairman. The branch members went on trips together, collected palm branches to cover succa roofs) to sell before the fall holiday of Succot, held a Purim carnival at school during the Hebrew month of Adar, and went to camp in the summer. Eliezer also kept a record of their activities and sent it to his older brother who was on Hachshara.

Yitz was proud of his younger brothers' activities and in a letter that he wrote to Eliezer in January, 1948, he indicated that he expected them to follow in his footsteps and to go on aliya to Eretz Yisrael. "Sooner or later, beyond all the socializing, fundraising and running around building a movement, you'll have to decide what all that means to you personally," he wrote. "For some, it's just a passing

event in their lives. Some will carry their Zionism like a hunchback for the rest of their lives. Others will settle for nothing less than the real thing, Palestine. Sooner or later, you'll face it. But, whatever the result, you can only be richer for the experience, and be a better Jew, too. In the meantime, enjoy it." But as happened in the end, Yitz stayed in Cleveland and established his family in America. He began to work in his father's company and helped him to expand it into a shop for recycling plastic.

After graduating high school, Eliezer and Jack went to study at Yeshiva University in New York. The yeshiva was founded in 1886 as a modern Orthodox institution that included in its undergraduate syllabus, very intensive Jewish studies. The students learned Judaism in the morning hours, followed by academic studies till 8PM. Jack's studies were even more challenging as he was studying pre-med. Eliezer decided quite early that his direction would be social work, so he chose to study sociology and psychology. From a young age he had decided to acquire a profession in which he would work with people. In an environment in which most young people were studying professions that were more lucrative, Eliezer's choice was considered unusual.

Eliezer was very happy for the many hours he was required to study Judaism and Hebrew at Yeshiva University. In a letter to his brother Yitz, from April, 1954, he wrote, "I'll never regret coming to Yeshiva University. This is my last chance for a solid, systematic Jewish education. Not the hit-and-run, death by doses of boredom-and-discipline of the Talmud Torah afternoon and Sunday school that we had in Cleveland, but serious courses and real teachers. I love it! It's not a hobby any more, but a vocation."

Eliezer confessed to his brother that within Jewish studies he was leaning more toward classes about the history and sociology of

Judaism than toward *halacha* (Jewish law), but he said, "One thing I swear even now! My children will know they are Jews and where they come from, and I'll do the best I can to help them keep faith with our past." He expressed dismay for the fact that the Hebrew names of his father and his brothers were changed to English. "This is the way we lose faith with our past, and lose our identity as Jews. I don't have the answer, other than guaranteeing our children a substantial Jewish education, but I am worried about what will be with us Jews in America fifty years from now. How will we know who we are?" He signed this letter to his big brother with a declaration that from now on and going forward he would only use his Jewish name, "Eliezer," and not the name "Lester," although a number of years went by until he changed his name formally. He began the letter to his brother with "Dear Arthur," but he let him know, at the end of the letter, that from now on he would call him "Yitz," short for "Yitzhak," and he would call his brother Jack by the name "Yaakov."

During their years of study in Yeshiva University, Eliezer and Jack didn't want to be financially dependent on their parents. "It's hard for us to ask for money since we both know how hard they work to earn it," wrote Eliezer to his brother Yitz, "but mostly because we just want to pull our own weight and not *shnorr*" (Yiddish for "beg"). In the beginning the brothers decided to save money by a diet they took upon themselves. They only ate bread, cheese and tuna. When they began to feel that this frugal nutrition was harming their health, they decided to find work in order to fund their studies. Eliezer and Jack noticed that most of the students in the dormitory ate their breakfast in their rooms and from there they ran to get to the first class at 8AM. Most of the students ate cereal for breakfast and they had to leave the dorm to buy milk in the nearby grocery store.

The brothers bought hundreds of milk cartons from a local dairy;

they would be brought to them at the building entrance at 5A.M., and they in turn would sell these cartons to the students at a profit of four cents per carton. It was a good idea but the work was hard. The student dorm was five stories high without an elevator and carrying the crates full of milk up the stairs to the students' rooms was not easy, especially for Eliezer, who did not have an especially sturdy body.

After a while, Eliezer and Jack came up with a new idea. They realized that their friends liked to eat breakfast while reading a newspaper. The two approached the marketing offices of the New York Times and the Herald Tribune and offered to deliver their papers to the students at the cost of three cents per newspaper. They would place the newspapers at the entrance of the students' rooms at 5:30 A.M. The profit from these jobs enabled Eliezer and Jack to diversify their meals and to enjoy some chicken, hamburger and soup.

At a certain point the hard work began to weigh them down, especially Eliezer, due to his back pain. To his delight, he received an offer of a new job. The dean of students, Professor Hyman Greenstein, invited him to a meeting and complimented him on his academic achievements in Jewish studies and Hebrew, "in spite of the fact that you were educated in Cleveland," and he asked Eliezer if he could give bar mitzva lessons to the wealthy director of a professional association, whose son was not able to read even one letter in Hebrew. The father decided that the time had come to give his son a meaningful Jewish education.

Eliezer was happy to accept the assignment. At the same time, he and Jack decided to transfer their milk line to other students and to make do with the distribution of newspapers, which were lighter to carry. In their studies and their work both brothers realized the philosophy of "Torah v'Avoda – Torah and Work" on which they had

been raised in their parents' home and in their youth movement.

On an April day in 1954, Eliezer and Jack were honored with a visit from their father. Henry Jaffe came to New York on business and used the opportunity to visit his two sons, the students, and to pamper them with a hot meal in a restaurant. That same night they hosted him in their dorm room. "You should have seen the look on the guys' faces," wrote Eliezer to his older brother Yitz, "as this short, fifty-seven-year-old, pot-bellied gentleman strolls down the corridor in my bathrobe and slippers, and showers leisurely with ten eighteen-year-olds alongside!"

With the completion of his studies at Yeshiva University, Eliezer returned to his parents' home in Cleveland and began studying at Western Reserve University in Cleveland, toward an M.A. in Social Work. He had been accepted to study law at a university in Chicago, but he preferred to continue his social work studies that spoke more to his heart. Two years later, when he concluded his studies in Cleveland, he took another degree in Criminology and Sociology at Ohio State University. From Ohio State, he returned to the university in Cleveland, and there he continued to a doctorate in social work, which he completed two months before making aliya.

## Chapter Two

## An Israeli Family

During his first year of teaching in the School of Social Work, Eliezer had a student named Rivka Schnerb. Rivka was born in 1932 in Frankfurt, Germany, to Chana Rachel and Chaim Gershon Schnerb. Her maternal grandfather, Louis Lamm, was a renowned and respected international Judaica collector, owner of a well-known shop in Berlin, during the first thirty years of the 20$^{th}$ century. Lamm was also the owner of a publishing company and during WWI he published a booklet on halacha for Jewish soldiers who were fighting at the front. Later he published some of the writings of Rabbi David Zvi Hoffman, among the leaders of German Jewry, who was known for his commentary on the Torah.

In 1934, shortly after the Nazis came into power, Lamm and his wife Julia and his young daughter Ruth moved to Amsterdam and left a great deal of his property and possessions in Berlin. The Nazis arrived in Holland in May, 1940, and that same year Julia Lamm died. In 1943, Louis Lamm and his daughter Ruth were sent together to a concentration camp in Holland and from there to Auschwitz, where they perished.

Chana Lamm, Rivka's mother, had not gone with her parents to Holland, nor did her brother Yisrael. They made aliya to Eretz

Yisrael and thus were saved from the Shoah. Chana made aliya in 1933 with her husband Chaim Gershon Schnerb and their two young daughters, Leah and Rivka. Two of Chaim Gershon's brothers had made aliya earlier. In Eretz Yisrael Rivka and her two sabra siblings, Rafi and Miriam, were born.

Chana had come from a wealthy family in Germany where she enjoyed a high standard of living, but in Eretz Yisrael, she lived with her husband and children in poverty, in a little hut in Petah Tikva. Her husband worked in the orchards and as a merchant, and she was a seamstress. Their financial situation was grim and forced her to sell her most expensive pieces of jewellery, but she never let her parents in Holland know about their situation.

In addition to seeing to the financial upkeep of the family, Chaim Gershon was also active in obtaining certificates that would enable his parents and three sisters to make aliya from Germany, and he succeeded in getting them out before the Shoah, but Chaim Gershon and Chana Schnerb did not succeed in getting out Chana's sister Ruth, and her father Louis (Yehuda), in time. Chaim and Chana were plunged into poverty so they could pay for the certificates, and the money was lost when Ruth and Louis were sent to their deaths before the certificates could reach them.

The financial hardships caused the Schnerb family to move from apartment to apartment within Petah Tikva and Bnei Brak. When Rivka was nine-years-old, the family moved to Jerusalem, to the poor, overcrowded Nahlaot neighborhood. Chana would buy used shoes for her children in the shuk, and clean them with kerosene, and the children were thrilled with the windfall. Rivka was acutely aware of the difficult financial situation of her parents and didn't ask them for anything, but she also had her red lines. Once, when she received used, shabby clothes from some relatives, she returned

them to their owners. Later she related that she did it from an internal desire to maintain her self-respect. "We may have lacked income but we didn't lack respect…"

In spite of the hardships, Chana and Chaim Gershon, who were part of the haredi-leumi stream of Poalei Agudat Yisrael (PAI), went to great efforts to give their children an education that was as religious and value-oriented as possible. Rivka and her older sister Leah studied in the Horev school in Jerusalem, and due to a low number of students, they were assigned to the same class. Along with their studies, Rivka was active in the Ezra youth movement, where she made many friends and had wonderful experiences.

When she was 14 years old, there was a turning point in Rivka's life. In order to help with the difficult financial situation in the home, she asked her Uncle Yitzhak Gross, who was the secretary general of the religious Hafetz Haim kibbutz, to register her in the group called "Eretz Yisrael Youth Program," who studied in the kibbutz in the framework of "Youth Aliya." The studies and life in kibbutz had a good influence on her. She met new friends, became more independent, and also was fortunate in being able to defend the kibbutz during the War of Independence.

When she was 17, she returned to Jerusalem and began to study in a course for practical nursing at Bikur Cholim Hospital. With the completion of her studies, Rivka began to work as a nurse in Tipat Halav (The national well baby clinic, or in English, "A Drop of Milk") in villages in the Jerusalem corridor. This was during the large aliyas to Israel, and Rivka helped many young mothers acclimate to their new land. In 1953 Rivka began to work as a family nurse in the Center for Community Health that was created by Hadassah in Beit Mazmil, in what came to be the Kiryat HaYovel neighborhood.

In her work in public health, Rivka encountered situations of

great emotional distress among many of her patients. Her feeling that she was lacking the tools and the skills to cope with the many challenges led her to the decision to expand her education and to study at the university. While still working, she completed her matriculation exams, and in 1960 she was accepted into the new School of Social Work at Hebrew University.

There the young new immigrant from America crossed paths with the Israeli nurse and social work student. The attractive and vibrant student found favor in the eyes of Eliezer. With time, he related that he found it difficult to concentrate both on her and on his lectures at the same time…their first meeting led rather quickly to a meaningful connection that became stronger with time. When Eliezer and Rivka got engaged, Rivka's fellow students wrote on the class blackboard: "Beauty and the Beast." The students were convinced that from then on, they would find that Rivka had all the answers to Dr. Jaffe's exams in advance, but of course they were disappointed. Eliezer, in his strict honesty, gave Rivka's exams to another lecturer to check.

Their wedding took place on Rosh Hodesh Elul, 5721, August 13, 1961, in a tourist club in Jerusalem. Rivka's father, Chaim Gershon, read a poem he wrote in honor of the young couple. "It is Rosh Hodesh today/To Jerusalem we have come/to bring joy to the bride and the groom. /Not just any groom/not just any bride/ I assume he was from America/ he came from afar/ Surely did not find someone there /For example, there are no girls there like Rivka/ There they all speak English and he likes Hebrew…"

In the beginning of their married life, the young couple lived in the faculty apartments of Hebrew University in the Hisahon (literally, "Savings") neighborhood in Bayit Vegan. They left their little home each day for the School of Social Work, where Eliezer would

teach and Rivka would study. Eliezer directed the development of the syllabus and the teaching of research in the new school. Those who were his students during that time period describe him as a lecturer who was modest, friendly and very accessible to students. From the beginning of his teaching career, he educated his students to include social activity in their framework of study. Dr. Baruch Ovadia, who founded and directed the Department of Social Welfare in the Ministry of Immigrant Absorption and Social Services, in Kupat Cholim Clalit (a health fund), was among Eliezer's students during his first year of teaching. Dr. Ovadia describes Eliezer as a teacher whose face lit up, who had a warm attitude to his students, who was organized and methodical. "The seminar in which I studied under him was about research methods. He suggested to us a number of methods and demonstrated also how they could be combined. He was not just a good lecturer and teacher in theory, but also related constantly to the practical angle, for he ascribed great importance to the profession of social work."

In spite of him being a new immigrant, during his second year of teaching Eliezer taught only in the Hebrew that he had acquired during his ulpan studies. New olim from the United States were uncommon in Israel in the early '60s. One day Eliezer received a letter from the Hadassah Medical Center, in which they requested that he participate in an international study on heart disease in Israel. The study compared the incidence of heart disease among Jews who were new immigrants to Israel to the level of morbidity among Jews who lived abroad. The letter explained to Eliezer that there were very few olim from America living in Israel, and therefore the researchers would be very happy if Eliezer would agree to participate in their study. Up until this very moment, we don't know what the results were of the study.

In the framework of his teaching in the university, Eliezer also interviewed candidates for the new School of Social Work, and he brought his worldview to this position also. One of the candidates was Zvi Feine, who later became the Deputy Director of the Joint Distribution Committee in Israel. Feine, like Eliezer, made aliya from America in 1960, but he was ten years younger than Eliezer. After a year of work at Kibbutz Yavne, Zvi decided to study social work and arrived for his interview.

He had failed the interview but received the option of an additional interview, this time with Eliezer, who not only accepted him, but also analyzed with him the mistakes he made in the first interview. The first mistake that Feine made, Eliezer explained, was that when he was asked if he would also study social work if he returned to the United States, Feine had replied that in America he would study economics and business administration, as they are more lucrative professions, and only because he was remaining in Israel did he want to study social work, for Zionistic reasons.

Feine's second mistake, according to Eliezer, occurred when he was asked, as a future social worker, if he would prefer working with a specific population group. Feine answered that he would prefer to not work with an older population but with children because, in his opinion, with younger people there was a higher chance of success for developmental and behavioral change. This was also an answer that the first interviewer did not approve of. In spite of this, in his second interview Eliezer decided to accept Feine and he said to him, "You are here for Zionistic reasons, you want to contribute to the State, we are looking for people like you and we will be happy to accept you."

Feine studied under Eliezer, and eventually even taught together with him in the School of Social Work. In spite of his initial

reluctance to work with an older population, his first job in social work was with the elderly and later he became chairman of the board of directors of ESHEL - the Association for the Planning and Development of Services for the Aged in Israel, a position he held for close to twenty years.

Rivka completed her B.A. in social work in 1962. Shortly after that, on Simhat Torah, Rivka and Eliezer gave birth to their oldest son, Uri Yehuda, and great joy filled their home. The Jaffe family overseas were all very emotional when they heard about the birth of their first Sabra grandchild. About a year later, Eliezer and Rivka and little Uri went to visit Cleveland, but for unhappy reasons. Henry, Eliezer's father, was diagnosed with cancer and when Eliezer heard about it, he decided that their little family would go together to visit his parents.

The family wanted to save Rivka and Eliezer the suffering of seeing his father dying and they thought it was better for them to stay in the home of one of the brothers. Only that evening, when Eliezer went to see his father for the first time, did he understand the seriousness of the situation. He returned agitated to the home of his brother and told him that he wanted to move in with his parents. Eliezer claimed that their mother, Sarah, needed the presence of the family around her as much as their father did.

Eliezer's father was very moved from the meeting with his son, his daughter-in-law and his little grandson. He gently touched the little hands of Uri and felt tremendous pride. Rivka, as an experienced nurse, volunteered to give Henry the painkilling shots every day. Shortly thereafter, on July 13, 1963, 21 Tammuz 5723, Henry Jaffe passed away, at the age of only 67. Many of the Jews in Cleveland came to accompany him on his final journey.

Next to the open grave, Eliezer and Yitz looked into each other's

eyes. They both knew that from now on Yitz would be the new head of the family, with everything that entailed. Yitz inherited not only the management of his father's company but also his wide-ranging activities in the Jewish community. He remained a passionate Zionist and continued to see the State of Israel as a modern miracle, but the family and communal responsibilities that he took upon himself in Cleveland diminished to an even greater degree the possibility that he would make aliya.

Four years after the death of Henry Jaffe, the young Israeli Jaffe family again came to Cleveland, this time for Eliezer's sabbatical year from the university. One of the reasons that Eliezer requested a sabbatical year was his desire to live with his family in Cleveland for a year, near his widowed mother. Since the previous visit, the Jaffe family expanded. To Uri was added a little sister named Yael, in February, 1965, Adar I, 5725.

When they arrived in Cleveland, Uri was four-years-old and Yael was a year and a half. Eliezer, Rivka and Yael lived in the same home together with Eliezer's mother, Savta Sarah Jaffe. The children of Eliezer's brothers were thrilled to meet their Sabra (Israeli born) cousins. In the course of the year, Eliezer taught in the School of Social Work and in the Department of Sociology in Cleveland, and worked in research. His work in the course of that year at the university was more intense than his work in Israel. Rivka improved her English, studied sewing, attended lectures on Judaism, and helped Eliezer in his research, but most of her time she dedicated to raising their two small children, who often got sick in the winter weather of Cleveland.

The sabbatical in Cleveland was a good opportunity for Rivka to get to know Eliezer's wider family. Every month there would be a family get together with all the cousins of Eliezer from his father's side, with all their children. "This is a wonderful idea," Rivka wrote

to her parents in Israel. "This way the entire family see each other and know what is going on with everyone. Today we will be meeting at the home of a cousin who is not at all religious and he ordered catering from a kosher restaurant and we'll eat on paper plates and with plastic flatware." Years later it was Rivka who took responsibility for organizing the family get-togethers of the Schnerb family.

In April, 1967, Sarah Jaffe received an award of distinction from the community for her wide-ranging contributions throughout the years to the shul and the community. At a ceremony in honor of the events, the rabbi of the community delivered an educational lecture, there was entertainment in Yiddish, and the entire community sang the song, "Eshet Chayil" ("Woman of Valor") and the anthems of the United States and Israel.

Eliezer received offers from local universities for the subsequent years, but he and Rivka were determined in their original plans to return to Israel at the end of the year. In March the Israeli student union in America asked Eliezer and Rivka to sign a declaration that their intention is to return to Israel at the end of the year. The intention of the union was to publicize the list of those who were returning to Israel in Israeli newspapers in reaction to the phenomenon of *yerida* – the leaving of Israel -- that became stronger during that time period.

Eliezer and Rivka did not sign the declaration, Rivka explaining it in a letter that she wrote to her parents. "We had the feeling that this activity is stupid since we do not have to declare before anyone our desire to return and whoever does declare it does not prove that he will really do so. In addition, we absolutely do not think that the situation is so bad that the only choice is to show the 'unfortunate' Israelis in Israel that we too, in the 'land of unlimited opportunities,' will also be returning.

"From among our friends many did not sign, especially those who knew for sure they would be returning to Israel, and they felt no need to demonstrate their desire to the wider public. Therefore, have no worries – we are coming home." Rivka expressed more than once her reservations from the group of *yordim* – those who had left Israel permanently – to settle in Cleveland. In one of her letters to her parents she wrote, "The number of yordim is growing and there are streets here where one can hear lots of Hebrew spoken. On the one hand we feel at home and on the other hand we feel repulsion towards the yordim. They of course say that they are all 'Israelis,' and we who will be returning are embarrassed when others identify us with them."

On Purim Eliezer and Rivka participated in a Purim party put on by the association of students and Israelis who came to the United States to study. Rivka chose to dress up as a poster calling for aliya to Israel. She pasted signs on herself about aliya, pictures of dollars, and wrote, 'Join those returning to the land of unlimited opportunities.' Eliezer, who was a fan of cartoons, dressed as Batman.

## Chapter Three

## Enlisting Without Being Called Up

The year was 1967. Yom Ha'atzmaut (Israeli Independence Day) - arrived and Rivka found it difficult to celebrate the national holiday outside of Israel. She decorated their home with Israeli flags and, together with the children, prepared little flags and a sign with the symbol of the State of Israel, but in the letter she wrote to her parents she spoke about the lack of joy and celebrations. "Our flag stood there lonely and embarrassed." Little Uri remembered the fireworks he would see in Israel and he cried when they explained to him that the holiday is not celebrated in Cleveland. Eliezer and Rivka were invited to a Yom Ha'atzmaut party organized by Israeli students but they didn't attend as it took place on the evening that was Yom Hazikaron (Memorial Day) in Israel. They were in America but their hearts were in Israel.

The winds of war began to blow in Israel. At the height of Israelis rejoicing on Yom Ha'atzmaut, Egyptian ground forces crossed the Suez Canal and entered the Sinai Desert. With that act, Gamal Abdel Nasser, the president of Egypt, plunged Israel into an emergency situation that was called "the waiting period." At the same time, in Northern Israel, the Syrians also began to speak of war. The atmosphere in Israel was tense and frightened. Citizens were required

to dig trenches, and the Rabbinate prepared spaces for thousands of graves.

As Israelis, Eliezer and Rivka felt isolated in the United States. It was very difficult for them to cope with the lack of information and the photographs of the capital cities of Arab countries that were screened on television. "I think it's much more frightening to hear about what is happening from afar," wrote Rivka to her parents, "without being able to do something – to volunteer in some way. Just to sit with our arms crossed in a wealthy country while our brothers and sisters are in trouble. It is not a simple thing."

One day Eliezer participated in a rally of support of Israel organized by one of the large synagogues in Cleveland. The speakers at the rally called, one after the other, to support Israel and to say verses of Psalms and Eliezer felt as if they were eulogizing Israel even before the war broke out. He left with a heavy heart before the rally was over and later he wrote in a letter to his brother Yitz, "Did they really think we Israelis were back in the ghetto going to the slaughter without a fight? It was they who were in the ghetto.

"And if they really thought we were at the brink, why were they sitting there in the synagogue, and not on their way to Israel? I know you may think it's naïve, but you fight wars with people and weapons, not with tears and Psalms. Everybody thinks that G-d, or Allah, or Jesus, is on his side in war and that boosts the troops' morale, and gives hope to parents and to the nations who are fighting. But beyond that you need soldiers, and plenty of them. You need proper equipment, and people to maintain it. The millions of dollars raised by Diaspora Jews during those emotional days were spent long *after* the war, not during. Where was all that tremendous wealth *before* the war? Did Jewish blood have to run before our needs were understood? And without those boys in Israel and their parents, and

the rest of us, there wouldn't be much of a Jewish state. Not before the war and not after."

But Eliezer was not just a talker but also a doer. He found it difficult to continue the Sabbatical in Cleveland when in Israel there was a war going on. Even before the war broke out, Eliezer began to check the possibilities of returning to Israel and being drafted. Two days before the war broke out, Rivka wrote to her parents, "Eli apparently will come [back to Israel] next week, since there are groups of students organizing and Israeli teachers who are returning to Israel. They were not called officially to go back but they are people who have no patience to sit and wait until something happens. Among them is Eli who is a real Zionist, 'Holier than the pope.' He has been very tense and feels that he has no place in Cleveland right now. So you'll be seeing him soon!"

On the day that the war began, Eliezer decided that he was flying to Israel the next morning to join the army. He wrote, "One of my very close relatives in Cleveland called me up that night and asked me not to go, begging me to think of my children and my wife, should anything happen to me. 'Stay here and help arrange for blood plasma, and meet with the press to tell the Israeli side of the story,' he said. That conversation made me even more upset and angry, and I asked him: 'Who do you think is going to fight for Rivka's mother, for Yael's classmates and for my students at the Hebrew University? Moshiach (the Messiah) all by himself?'"

As Eliezer left for Israel, Rivka wrote a letter to her parents in which she described the reaction of his family to his decision. "Everyone was proud of him, the pioneer, but you have no idea how much they opposed his going and what things they said to me for not stopping him. It was not at all obvious to them, that a person has to do what he needs to do for his country. They are the unfortunate

ones. They don't know the feeling of living in our land, with our government, where we don't have to be afraid to say what we think. "Even in a democracy like the United States there is a lot that is not said or done due to the fear, 'What will the goyim say?' They don't understand how someone would go of his own free will and join the army, just as they don't understand that a Jew, because he is an American citizen, needs to fight in Vietnam. They think about that and mistakenly compare their feelings to their country here [that is hosting them]. And they think that this should be their feeling also toward Israel. Eli proved himself as a real Zionist and I am very, very proud of him. May G-d keep him safe and may a hair of his head not fall to earth, metaphorically, since every day he gets more and more bald…" She continued, "Tell Eli that his mother feels fine – she is proud of him even if she can't say it to me."

Eliezer arrived in Israel on the third day of the war at 5 A.M. and went quickly to the deployment center. The sergeant who received him there said to him, "We'll call you when we need you" and sent him home, but Eliezer was still happy that he had come home to Israel. When he got to Jerusalem, he went to visit his friend Dr. Israel Katz, head of the department of Social Work at Hebrew University, who was also waiting to be called up by the army.

In the days that followed Eliezer volunteered in the School for Social Work and elsewhere. Among other things, he would use his car to take sick people to Hadassah Hospital in Jerusalem.

The war ended with a stunning victory of Israel over her enemies, and with a significant expansion of the state's borders. The Old City of Jerusalem was liberated and, with her, the Temple Mount and the Kotel. Eliezer traveled through the territories that were liberated in the Jordan Valley and in Gush Etzion. He visited Ma'arat Hamachpela (Cave of the Patriarchs), the Tomb of Rachel, and of course the

Kotel. In a letter that he wrote to his brother Yitz he described the high emotion while visiting the Kotel. "The Old City that has been revealed to us is like from another world…The constant flow of Jews making their way to the Kotel is unbelievable! After two thousand years and after all the efforts of the Babylonians, Greeks, Romans, Moslems, Crusaders, Turks, Nazis, British and Arabs to destroy us and prevent us from establishing our homeland, we stand again in the Temple of Solomon. It's hard to believe we are participating in these events in our own lifetime. Yesterday I touched those giant Herodian stones and I thought about our father who didn't merit to arrive here until now. I also thought about the hundreds of years of Jewish prayers to reach this day and for this place. You must see this with your own eyes."

About three weeks after the war ended, Eliezer returned to Cleveland. In a letter that Rivka wrote to her parents upon his return, she told them about the change that had occurred in Eliezer's mood in the wake of his visit to Israel. "He returned in good spirits, quiet and calm, more than when he left. During those weeks of [pre-war] tension and on the eve of the war he was so agitated and it was difficult to talk to him…he didn't play with the children and would only sit and listen to the radio and watch the TV news and he felt uncomfortable that he was here at this time of trouble in Israel. Thank G-d that everything played out as it did, it is only a shame that so many were killed or wounded in the process."

Eliezer brought back slides of the places that had been liberated during the war, a Jordanian flag that he found in Kfar Etzion, stones that he gathered in Jericho and a glass vase from Hebron. Three days after his return to Cleveland, Eliezer and Rivka invited family members to a special evening where he showed the slides, exhibited the articles he had brought from Israel and related his experiences.

A few days later Eliezer and Rivka hosted a similar evening to which they invited Israelis who live in Cleveland. At that evening, Eliezer also played radio news programs that were broadcast during the war, that he had recorded into his tape recorder in real time. The Israelis reacted with great excitement. The rumors of Eliezer's presentations took wing and he was invited by a number of organizations to give talks about the war.

Eliezer and his family returned to Israel at the end of August, 1967, two months after the war. They did not return to their rented apartment in Bayit Vegan but to a new apartment at 37 Azza [Gaza] Road in the Rehavia neighborhood, which they had bought before they went to Cleveland. With his return to Israel, Eliezer put in a request to the Ministry of Interior to change his name officially from "Lester" to "Eliezer." The university published a letter in September, 1967, in which they wrote, "Dr. Jaffe requests to call him by his Hebrew name: Eliezer Yaffe." At the end of a year during which he had proved what an enthusiastic Zionist he was, by returning to Israel to participate in the war, Eliezer made his Israeli mark also by changing his first name.

In December, 1967, half a year after the war, Yitz accepted his younger brother's invitation and came to Israel for the first time. He landed two days before Chanuka and the brothers spent ten days together. Eliezer and Rivka took Yitz to Masada and to the Dead Sea, to Kfar Etzion, to the Israel Museum, to Mea She'arim and to the Kotel. Yitz also joined Eliezer on a trip down south where Eliezer spoke before soldiers, in the framework of his reserve duty.

Yitz was very moved to see his younger brother wearing the IDF uniform. Eliezer reminded Yitz that twenty years earlier he was the one who looked up to his older brother with admiration when Yitz was planning to make aliya and join the IDF, during his time on the

Hachshara of Hashomer Hadati in New Jersey. Yitz tremendously enjoyed the warm hospitality of his brother and his sister-in-law and his visit to Israel aroused and strengthened the Zionist feelings that were always within him. "In spite of everything I read and the albums that I flipped through, I could not appreciate Israel without seeing her with my own eyes and without breathing her atmosphere, especially on Chanuka," he wrote to Eliezer as soon as he returned to Cleveland.

During that time period, seven years after Eliezer had made aliya, he put in an official request to the Ministry of Interior to receive Israeli citizenship. Until then he had avoided obtaining Israeli citizenship because when he made aliya he was told that olim from America were obligated to give up their American citizenship in order to be Israeli citizens. In December, 1967, Eliezer sent a letter to Minister Haim-Moshe Shapiro, the Minister of Interior, in which he requested to receive Israeli citizenship but to also allow him to keep his American citizenship. Eliezer explained that his request was due to family and financial reasons. "In Cleveland, Ohio, I left an elderly widow, who has still not made her peace with my aliya and with the fact that I left my homeland and my American family, and especially after the passing away of my father, of blessed memory, a number of years ago. I must respect my mother's wishes, and visit her to comfort her to and to help her, when necessary, to get used to her new life following the death of my father. In addition, I do not want to disconnect from the legal connection I have with my mother's affairs and to endanger everything involved with my responsibilities toward her.

"I believe that the loss of my American citizenship may make it difficult for me to help my mother," Eliezer explained in his letter. He also explained that he needed American citizenship in order to

take proper care of his parents' finances and assets. In addition, he claimed that from the professional perspective, his American citizenship would enable him to receive fellowships, research positions, and research grants that were only available to American citizens. "I believe that I can contribute much more to our country and to my professional development by keeping both citizenships," he wrote. He concluded his letter to the minister with an honest declaration. "My identification with the State of Israel is not dependent on my receiving the agreement to my request, as I have already put down deep roots in Israel and have arrived at the conclusion that I must fully join with the fate of my people in Israel. Therefore, I plan on requesting Israeli citizenship even if you will reject my request to maintain both citizenships. It would just be a real shame for the personal and professional difficulties that I will encounter, if there is a negative response to my request."

Several months later Eliezer received a letter from the minister in which he was told that his request was granted and he would receive a certificate of Israeli citizenship that would indicate he is a full Israeli citizen. To Eliezer's joy, the minister also removed the demand that Eliezer relinquish his American citizenship.

At the end of October, 1967, the appointments committee of the university recommended that Eliezer be promoted to the position of senior lecturer in the School of Social Work. During the same time period the school still did not have one professor and all the senior lecturers were assessed by professors from other departments. Eliezer's promotion was, for the most part, due to the important research projects he had accomplished during those years.

One study that he directed, on the topic of keeping young people in institutions for youth and how to help them integrate anew into their homes, was the first study done in the School of Social Work

and it had a direct influence on social welfare policy in Israel. In the context of the study, Eliezer exposed, among other things, the many defects in the services that were given to the young people in these institutions, and the exposure of this situation angered more than a few people from the social service establishment.

Like the rest of his colleagues, Eliezer was forced to cope with a disrespectful attitude that existed in Israel toward social workers. Most of the social workers who worked in Israel at that time did not have academic training. They were graduates of an institute for the preparation of social workers that was directed by the Ministry of Welfare. The establishment did not appreciate them. They related to them as if they were good people, who could be easily replaced by any other person with good intentions, even without professional training.

Social workers began to be related to differently when the first graduates of the School of Social Work entered the work force. Gradually, Israeli society also began to understand the importance of academic training for social workers, and the status of the social workers began to slowly improve. Another thing that contributed to the improvement of their status was the establishment of departments of social work in additional universities. As a result of the success of the School of Social Work in Jerusalem, Tel Aviv University, Haifa University and Bar Ilan University also opened departments of social work and the process contributed to strengthening the status of the profession.

The change in the status of the social workers was also reflected in the establishment of a professional association, and Eliezer played a crucial role in this change. From the time he arrived in Israel, Eliezer was bothered by the fact that the union of social workers that operated in the framework of the Workers' Union was not part of the

academic sector of the union but part of the office workers' sector. This reality more and more disturbed Eliezer's peace of mind as the number of social workers with academic degrees grew. In order to change the situation, Eliezer began to work together with some of his colleagues and former students to create a new professional union for social workers that would compete with the existing union. Something else about the existing union that bothered Eliezer and his friends was its connection to political parties. The process of elections in the union institutions was based on the list of candidates who were there on behalf of political parties. Members of the union would not vote for specific candidates, but for political parties, and the parties that received the most votes received the most places in the union institutions.

Eliezer was convinced that the social work profession could not be conducted in this way. Together with his friends in the new union, they demanded, from the Histadrut and the government, the power to administer elections that were based on the personal achievements of the candidates and not on their membership in one party or another. The members of the new union elected Eliezer to be their leader and he became more and more involved in the policy and strategy of the professional union. Histadrut HaOvdim, the veteran union of social workers and of government offices, did not like this organizing, but the social workers "voted with their feet" and joined the new union in droves, paid membership dues, and encouraged Eliezer and his friends.

The revolt succeeded. Shortly afterwards, the Histadrut fired the chairman of the Histadrut, who herself had no academic education in the field. The Histadrut members promised Eliezer and his members of the new union that the next chairman of the Social Workers' Union would be professionally educated and elections would not be

held on the basis of political parties. The Histadrut also undertook to open negotiations for the transfer of the Social Workers Union to the Histadrut's Academic Division. Eliezer felt great satisfaction. In a letter to his brother Yitz he wrote: "[T]here is a promise of allowing personal elections – for the first time in Histadrut history – and for negotiations to transfer our union to the Academic Division of the Histadrut. Now that's real satisfaction! You watch and see, in a few more years, the young graduates will take over their union completely, and turn it into a force for social policy and social services, and for better work conditions for social workers. They can do more good for Israel than people can imagine.

"I've been bitten by the social action bug, and I'm trying to find a role for myself that can combine academic work with advocacy and change. I can't just preach change to students, and report on the need for change found in my research projects, without getting involved myself. That's my dilemma right now, and I'll have to find a solution somehow. Love to you and the family, Eli"

The solution was implemented not long after.

## Chapter Four

## From University to the Jerusalem Municipality

A surprising phone call came in 1970 from the office of Jerusalem Mayor Teddy Kollek. During the meeting, Eliezer was asked if he would be willing to head the municipality's Welfare Department. To an outside observer, the appeal to Eliezer was very surprising. Up until that time, people who were assigned to that position identified with a particular political identity and party affiliation within the municipal system. This was the first time the position had been offered to an academic, a candidate outside the political and municipal system. Beyond that, the invitation to Eliezer was surprising for another reason. Eliezer and his colleagues at the School of Social Work were considered the biggest critics of government and municipal welfare departments.

In January 1970, a few months before Eliezer was approached, a lengthy article was published in the Maariv newspaper in which Eliezer and his colleagues sharply criticized the welfare services in Israel, which they claimed suffered from inefficient organizational structure, deficiencies in their social perception, and competition between party and government institutions.

Eliezer claimed in the article that the main deficiency in the welfare services in Israel lay in the fact that the disadvantaged public

throughout the country do not know what their rights are, do not receive the guidance they deserve, and especially do not receive the minimum rights in a dignified and effective manner. Eliezer also told Maariv reporter Yosef Tzuriel that in Israel there is terrible neglect in the field of personal and human treatment of the disadvantaged, and he pointed an accusing finger at the municipal welfare departments.

"Until now, no welfare authority has published a booklet in which you explain in simple Hebrew what a large family deserves, what help a single widow is entitled to, who deserves a certain grant, and to whom one turns when they need to clarify a problem. Failure to publish such a booklet," said Eliezer, "is not a trivial thing. It indicates that here in Israel, only someone who knows to reach out receives help, and even then, the help is not given as a right, but as support of the strong for the weak."

Eliezer also claimed that the fact that the welfare services had the distorted perception that what they were providing to the needy was a *hesed*, a favor, rather than a right, left the social workers invisible, in their offices. "This is the convenient way for a government to gives its benevolence to the public who are in need."

Eliezer argued that in the reality that has been created, the beneficiaries also needed legal advice from a neutral body because it was difficult to expect welfare workers in local authorities and the government to give advice to those in need on how to act *against* the institutions in which they worked.

Eliezer's critique did not end there. A few months after the article was published in Maariv, the head of the Jerusalem municipality's personnel department arrived at the university's School of Social Work in order to recruit the school's graduates to the municipality's Welfare Department. He lectured on the many jobs awaiting staff, the department's great need for social workers and the significant

career that awaited new employees. Eliezer came to the meeting out of curiosity but the words of the senior official in the municipality angered him greatly.

Eliezer wrote to Yitz, "I sat in on the meeting out of curiosity, but got so angry at the nonsense he was handing out that I asked to speak. I told him and the students that anybody who works under the conditions that exist, and with the professional constraints imposed on staff, ought to have his head examined. I suggested that instead of trying to recruit young graduates to run the services, he ought to concentrate on changing the Welfare Department so that it would be worthy of attracting students."

Apparently, Eliezer's sharp words fell on attentive ears. He wrote to Yitz, "Soon after that episode I got a call from my old friend and former student, Yaakov Gil, now a senior official in the City's Department of Sport and Culture and the deputy-chairman of the Union of City Employees. He is also well plugged into the mayor's party, which doesn't hurt. Yaakov asked if I'd be interested in discussing the Welfare Department job with the head of Personnel. Several meetings later, and feeling that they would let me fool around with streamlining the department, I was invited for a chat with the mayor.

"I must say that one of the things which attracted me to the job was the mayor himself. I had rooted for his election as an independent who bolted his party (Labor) and I liked his frankness, although not his impetuous temper which was unfitting for a public personality. Seated in his big chair behind a long desk, he looked at me above his bi-focal eyeglasses to size me up."

In his meeting with Kollek, he was under the impression that the mayor had already decided to accept him for the post. Most of the questions at the meeting were asked by Deputy Mayor Rabbi Menachem Porush, who held the welfare portfolio. Eliezer stressed

at the meeting that he would agree to be on loan from the university for only two years and also requested that his salary be the same salary he received from the university. In doing so, Eliezer sought to maintain his independence and allow him to leave the position, if he felt he was not being allowed to perform his job properly. Eliezer also referred to his work at the municipality as a "laboratory of experiments" and saw this as another reason to maintain his independence. "You can only run a lab when you are the head of the lab and you do not need favors," he explained.

Eliezer wrote to Yitz, "You know, before I took this job, I asked my colleagues at the university what they thought about the idea. One outstanding, emeritus professor of education said I'd be making a mistake, that civil service work was inherently opposed to change, and that the university certainly wouldn't appreciate it anyhow. One social work teacher was surprised and simply jealous that I had been asked to take the job. Another was delighted that the School of Social Work would now have some 'protektzia' (influence) in the welfare offices for research and student field placements. And still another faculty person thought I was out of my mind to interrupt academic work and teaching 'to go into the field.' Who is right?"

Eliezer saw in this new position an opportunity to implement the "bug of social activism" that had been within him throughout his ten years of academic work.

When Eliezer received the official contractual offer for the position of Director of the Welfare Department, he discussed it at length with Rivka. Just seven months earlier, on the eve of Rosh Hashana, 5733, twin girls were born to the young Jaffe family: Naomi and Ruti. Yael was five-years-old and Uri was eight-years-old. The significance of taking on this new position would mean lengthy absences from home for Eliezer, and a heavier burden on Rivka. However, Rivka

knew how important it was to Eliezer to return to professional work in the field, and expressed her willingness for him to take on this new challenge, which was defined from the beginning as limited to two years.

Eliezer wrote, "Jerusalem's social problems are getting much worse as the city grows larger. Some of the increased poverty, use of drugs, teenage prostitution and street corner life, is directly related to the aftermath of the Six-Day War."

About one-sixth of the families in Jerusalem were treated by the Welfare Department. An article published in the Haaretz newspaper about the social problems in the capital read: "On the periphery of the city, the reality is miserable. Children are sleeping in cramped conditions in a room filled with beds, the food in the home is meager, youth gangs flee their crowded homes, develop habits of violence that quickly turn to crime…researchers discerned that there are families in Jerusalem who are living in desolate lifestyle conditions for two generations."

One of the things that particularly troubled Eliezer was the correlation that existed between socio-economic problems and ethnic origin. He was aware that it was difficult for people to hear this, but he could not ignore the fact that the poor population in Jerusalem was mostly of Sephardic descent. "This Ashkenazi-Sephardi (Western vs. Middle-Eastern Jews) polarity is extremely dangerous," he wrote to Yitz, "and I can't understand how naïve and passive the Sephardi leadership here is. It's unbelievable how they have accepted the Ashkenazi stereotypes and priorities. If the Sephardi 'establishment' outside of Israel knew how serious things are, they would be shocked." The ethnic issue would continue to seriously occupy Eliezer in the coming years.

One of Eliezer's great challenges, immediately upon becoming

the director of the Jerusalem Welfare Department, was improving the status and image of the department's social workers. He was saddened to discover the harsh working conditions of the employees who worked in cramped offices, with very little privacy and that they were forced to handle a huge case load. Each employee in the department was required to care for more than two hundred families. Eliezer was also under the impression that the status of social workers among all municipal workers was at the bottom of the ladder. One of Eliezer's first actions was to paint the department's offices in various branches in the city, and to have curtains hung in their rooms. He believed that improving the external appearance of the offices might improve both the image of the department and the self-image of its employees. He was angered by the implicit assumption that social workers do not need nice offices because they serve clients from weak populations.

Eliezer also made a small change in his new office. He replaced the old wooden chair assigned to him with a new chair. It never occurred to him that this little replacement would be considered excessive by someone. A few weeks after taking office he came to the city treasurer to ask for a budget to install a heating system in one of the department's branches that was undergoing renovations. Eliezer told the treasurer that without central heating, social workers and customers will suffer badly from the Jerusalem cold, and there is no reason to discriminate against them while employees in other departments in the municipality already enjoy central heating in their offices.

The treasurer's response stunned Eliezer. Not only did he object to the financing of the heating for the workers but he also attacked Eliezer personally for daring to replace the chair in his office. "How come you bought that fancy chair," he said. "Wasn't the old chair

good enough for you?" This is the question the treasurer asked as he sat on a luxurious velvet chair with a raised backrest. Eliezer was stunned by the treasurer's response. He returned agitated to his office, and after a short time hired the services of a sturdy porter and had him carry his new chair directly to the treasurer's office. He attached a note to the chair in which he wrote: "Please accept the attached chair with my compliments. When you sit in it for a while, perhaps you'll better understand the problems of the Welfare Department."

Twenty minutes later, the porter returned the chair to Eliezer's office. Attached to the chair was a new note in which it was written in the treasurer's handwriting: "Returned with thanks. No offence meant." The treasurer understood the message that Eliezer wanted to convey to him and in the end also supplied a budget for central heating for the renovated branch of the social workers. Eliezer saw in this case a clear illustration that a change in the status of social workers can be brought about, if only they stand firm on their rights and preserve their dignity.

One of the first steps Eliezer took in his position was to change the name of the department from the Welfare Department, or its official name: "Department of Social Work" to "Department of Family and Community Services." By changing the name, Eliezer expressed his desire to change the image of the department, from a department that deals with charity, to a department that takes care of solving social problems and empowering family and community. In the end, the attempt to get the public used to the new department name did not go well. The media continued to call it, "The Social Department." However, the demand to change the name of the Welfare Department and also the name of the Ministry of Welfare in the government, was accepted by the public after a number of years. In

1977, the Ministry of Welfare was merged with the Ministry of Labor and has since been called the Ministry of Labor and Social Welfare.[3] Shortly after taking office Eliezer faced the limitations of his role. The vast majority of the budget of the Welfare Department was allocated to issues set by the government. Eliezer realized that he could make the budget work more efficiently in certain areas to which it had already been allocated, and try to initiate new actions with the rest of the budget.

Upon taking office, Eliezer wrote to his brother, "I have a funny feeling that, although lack of money is a big problem in welfare work, my biggest problem may turn out to be converting people to a more humane and rational conception of social goals and social work. That's much harder to do than raising money, but in the long run, it's the most critical task."

In an interview with Haaretz a few weeks after taking office, Eliezer said that the treatment of the underprivileged population consists of three areas: values, means, and execution. "First, the prevailing values in society must be changed and it must be recognized that urgent treatment of social problems are crucial to that society. Then this change in values must be reflected in the budget, and finally, there must be effective implementation of welfare policies that are funded by society." He told reporter Uzi Benziman that he felt there had been a positive change in values with Mayor Teddy Kollek and expressed hope that the change would also be reflected in the increase in resources.

Another step initiated by Eliezer was the reorganization of the municipal welfare bureaus and the accessibility of the various

---

[3] Today it is called the Ministry of Labor, Social Affairs, and Social Services.

services to citizens. Prior to Eliezer commencing his position, seven regional bureaus operated in Jerusalem, but many services were provided only at the department's management offices in the city center. Eliezer reduced the number of regional bureaus to only four but significantly expanded their areas of activity. Services previously provided only at the department's main offices began to be provided at the regional offices as well.

In addition, the responsibilities and independence of the employees in the regional bureaus were expanded and the number of cases submitted for the care of each employee was reduced. At the same time, Eliezer established a new bureau for planning and research, added free legal advice to the disadvantaged within the regional bureaus, and tripled the number of social workers in educational institutions in order to prevent students from dropping out of school.

Eliezer also opened a new unit in the Welfare Department for care of the elderly. In order to locate all the elderly in the city who needed assistance, Eliezer instructed the social workers in the field to report to the department every elderly person in the families cared for by them, and also asked the city residents to report to the department every elderly person in their neighborhood who needed assistance. After the new unit began its activities, it became clear that forty per cent of those being served by the department were elderly, and two thirds of the elderly treated by the department were below the poverty line.

Another revolutionary move made by Eliezer was publishing a booklet listing the rights of the residents of the city. The booklet enabled those in need to see if and how much the department's regional bureaus could help them or their relatives who needed help. The booklet indicated who was entitled to financial support, the welfare quota, how the number of persons eligible for support is

calculated, and to what level of support they are entitled, how help from the bureau can be obtained, what documents are needed to obtain that help, what are the obligations of those who are aided by the department and how decisions can be appealed.

Aaron Payne worked during this time period in the Family and Community Services Department and he was the one asked by Eliezer to write the booklet listing these rights. According to him, the publication of the pamphlet was considered revolutionary at the time. "People were unaware of their rights, and this was a convenient reality for the state institutions because there were fewer demands. Eliezer strived for transparency and of course was not concerned that the publication of the booklet would lead to a flood of inquiries from the disadvantaged. He said that the system will cope and will know how to organize and to give the services that are coming to those who turn to it."

Eliezer was due to end his two-year term in April 1972, but a few weeks before his termination, he was fired by Mayor Teddy Kollek. Tensions between Eliezer and the mayor began about a year earlier, around the establishment of the Black Panthers protest movement.

The "Black Panthers" was a movement founded by young people from the Musrara neighborhood of Jerusalem whose parents immigrated to Israel from North Africa. The young peoples' goal was to protest against the discrimination of the Sephardim in the country, and in March, 1971, they initiated a demonstration in front of the Jerusalem municipality.

Ahead of the demonstration, Mayor Teddy Kollek convened an urgent meeting of city department heads and city council members to discuss how to treat the Panthers and the expected demonstration. Most of the speakers in the room expressed concern about the ethnic tensions created by the protest and feared the impact of the

demonstration on the image of the State of Israel. Eliezer, who had previously warned of the consequences of ethnic disparities, and one of the city council members who was of Sephardic descent, were the only two people in the meeting who suggested the mayor recognize the Panthers and open a dialogue with them to calm the atmosphere. The rest of the speakers advised the mayor to act against the Panthers and conduct a campaign in the city neighborhoods against participating in the demonstration.

Eliezer expressed support for the Panthers' organizing and said so also in the Knesset's Education and Public Services Committees, to which he was summoned to discuss the issue of youth in distress. He said at the hearing that organizing is positive and healthy because people and youth in distress must organize to get out of their predicament, even though it involves politicizing the ethnic feeling. In addition, Eliezer also criticized the government ministries' handling of the issue of youth in distress and argued that legislation was needed that would make providing social services mandatory and not optional. The Ministry of Welfare expressed resentment and reservations about what Eliezer said in the Knesset.

The police refused to give the Panthers permission to demonstrate. After they decided to demonstrate anyway, and also to protest the refusal to let them demonstrate, the police arrested their leaders for questioning. Eliezer believed that the refusal to hold the demonstration was a mistake. He wrote to his brother Yitz, "How scared and idiotic can you get? It's hard for me to believe that the police did all this on their own without discussing it with the government, city hall, or the prime minister. The establishment was so out of touch with what was going on that they would not tolerate a hint of genuine ethnic problems, even though we had absorbed, in only 23 years, people from 120 countries, speaking over 70 different languages, and

nearly 800,000 of them were Jews from Arab countries."

Eliezer was also frustrated that, throughout the affair, no government or municipal official consulted with the municipality's social workers who knew the area and the people working in the Panther movement. The mayor and his people not only did not think of consulting the social workers, but even accused them of aiding the Panthers in their protest. To prevent the workers from contacting the Panthers, the mayor and his deputy decided to make a "divide and conquer" move and transfer the section of community work from the Welfare Department run by Eliezer to the Education Department which was more closely controlled by the deputy mayor.

This move created a disconnect between the community social workers and the rest of the social workers, prevented cooperation between them and harmed the functioning of the Welfare Department. There was no one to talk to, and a real conspiracy existed to shut up both the Panthers and the social workers as well. The accusations against Eliezer came not only from the municipality. Eliezer told his brother that a sociologist from the Hebrew University accused him of establishing the Black Panthers with the aim of creating social change.

Reuven Abergel, one of the leaders of the Black Panthers protest movement' says today that contrary to the claims made at the time, Eliezer did not help organize a protest and did not push him and his friends to fight. However, Abergel says, unlike all the representatives of the establishment at the time, Eliezer did not delegitimize the members of the Panthers and did not see them as a disturbing force, but rather showed empathy for them and saw their social activity as a potential for positive change.

"For us he was the right man in the right place. Unlike others, his door was always open for us. We found him willing to give a shoulder

to social action, and he actually helped us find creative solutions to the difficult reality that existed at the time in the neighborhoods. For example, he obtained a budget for buses on which we could send children from the neighborhoods to summer camps and trips. He understood that activists like us could help him obtain resources and tools for implementing social ideas." While Prime Minister Golda Meir then described the Panthers as "not nice," Eliezer, Abergel says, expressed warmth towards him and his friends. "Unlike others, he spoke to us in respectful language. In meetings with him you were not meeting with an alienated city official but with a person who knows how to say a good word to you and give you advice on how to improve your social action."

The Black Panthers protest created a crisis of confidence between Mayor Kollek and Eliezer but the crisis intensified more significantly later, around the budget issue for the department. Eliezer and the department's senior staff built a new program designed to provide assistance to the department's clients under a section defined as "other assistance" and included special needs that the regular welfare budget could not solve. The "other assistance" included items such as health care expenses, educational expenses and home help expenses. Because the budget for this assistance was limited, and provided on the basis of "first come, first served," funding for certain types of needs ended long before the end of the fiscal year of 1971. Social workers decided not to wait for a new fiscal year but to demand an immediate budget increase.

Eliezer, for his part, also submitted a request for an expanded budget to the mayor. Both the mayor and the Ministry of Welfare objected to providing additional funds and as a result, the action committee set up by the social workers following the crisis declared a strike.

On the morning of the strike, Eliezer was summoned to the city treasurer, who informed him that a source had been found to finance the additional budget. The mayor suspected Eliezer was the one who planned the workers' protest and strike. His suspicion stemmed from the fact that some of Eliezer's colleagues at the university were active on the action committee. In reality, Eliezer actually showed loyalty to the municipality and did not meet with the workers' action committee during the protest.

In November, 1971, an in-depth article was published in the newspaper Davar about the Welfare Department in Jerusalem. "Dr. Jaffe has chalked up some impressive achievements within a year," wrote journalist Nahum Barnea. "The number of professional workers has increased by scores. Budgets were doubled, a reorganization of the department has ensued, and most importantly, clear and precise criteria were formulated - for the first time in Israel - for the distribution of funds for assistance beyond the elementary welfare support." The article claimed that one of the reasons the budget of the Welfare Department ended before the fiscal year was over was due to the booklet listing the rights that Eliezer published, that caused people defined as disadvantaged, who were not previously aware of their rights, to approach the department.

In February, 1972, towards the end of the fiscal year 1971, a discussion began on the budget for the new year. It became clear to Eliezer that the budget earmarked for that year would not allow the department to implement its work properly. Since his two-year term in the municipality would end in April in any case, Eliezer decided to move up the end to his term and to submit his resignation to the mayor. He refused to act on a meager budget and to bear the social consequences. Shortly after submitting his resignation, Eliezer received a call from a senior city official, demanding that he retract his

resignation and even threatening that if he did not do so, he would blacken his name in the media.

Since a year later municipal elections were to be held, the mayor's concern was that the resignation of the director of the Welfare Department would damage the municipality's image before the elections. Eliezer refused to retract his resignation, and since the senior employee spoke rudely to him, he even slammed down the phone in the middle of the call. Eventually things calmed down, and at a city council meeting in early March the mayor even had warm words of farewell in praise of Eliezer for the way he had run the department.

Eliezer was appeased and thought the storm was behind him. He planned to end his term on time, in early April, and believed that the last month of his term would run smoothly, but the crisis between him and the mayor erupted again and reached its peak shortly thereafter.

This time the relationship exploded for another reason. Several months earlier, there was a suspicion in the Welfare Department of the municipality that funds that were supposed to reach the department from the Ministry of Welfare had not reached their destination. Eliezer turned to the municipal comptroller and asked him to investigate the matter. In early March the municipal comptroller presented to the municipality's finance committee the report he had compiled following Eliezer's request.

It turned out that the funds that the department was entitled to from the Ministry of Welfare had been delayed by the treasury of the municipality. It also turned out that if the money would have reached the department, they could have operated much more efficiently. Eliezer read the conclusions of the report before the finance committee of the city. Out of satisfaction that the Welfare Department had been right and been made public, he also made sure to

send copies of the report to all of his department's senior staff.

Eliezer wrote to his brother, "Then all hell broke loose. The next day, banner headlines appeared in Maariv: 'Jerusalem Municipality Comptrollers' Report: Three Million Pounds Earmarked for the Welfare Department Swallowed in the General Municipal budget.' Then followed a complete summary of the comptroller's report, blaming the Treasury and completely supporting my earlier claims. Around 5:00 P.M. this afternoon, as I worked alone in my office, I got a phone call from the mayor, all fire and brimstone. He shouted that the Maariv article had besmirched the administration's good name, and how could I send copies of the comptroller's report to my staff, since the report is an internal (!) document? I told him to calm down and meet with me to discuss the matter, but he was so riled up he wouldn't hear my side of it. After a volley of choice English swear-words he told me to stop my work and that I was dismissed. I reminded him that I had already resigned and had twenty days to go to April 1$^{st}$, and suggested that if the city's image bothered him, he should calm down and think. But his temper was out of bound and he could only repeat his demand that I leave. I quietly told him: 'I think you're wrong, but you're the boss,' and I gathered up my personal belongings and left."

The next day, the news of Eliezer's firing by telephone was published in the newspapers. The mayor confirmed the news and justified the dismissal by saying that Eliezer acted in violation of all accepted administrative rules when distributing the comptroller's report. Eliezer refrained from commenting on the dismissal and only said that the mayor's announcement was impulsive and did not address the problems of the Welfare Department. Journalist Yosef Tzuriel wrote in Maariv that the way in which the mayor chose to fire Eliezer, "made Dr. Jaffe a 'martyr' who wins the affection of the

employees of the Welfare Department and of the social workers in Jerusalem."

And indeed, Kollek's behavior toward Eliezer agitated the Welfare Department workers. They assembled and decided to shut down all department services in protest. In addition, they sent a telegram to the mayor demanding that he apologize to Eliezer, return him to work by the end of the month and hold a meeting with them in the light of the municipal auditor's report. The mayor condemned their strike but met with them and in the meeting apologized for the way in which he had fired Eliezer. They returned to work the next day.

Eliezer wrote to Yitz, "You know, the ironic part is that I really liked the mayor and wanted to make him the national model as a pioneer and patron of the social services. But he's basically a mortar and brick man, and terribly impulsive. Social services are hard to see and hard to sell, and some leaders cannot grasp that admitting the existence of social problems is the first step to dealing with them, and even to getting funds for the job. The fear of being 'blamed,' of being thought of as incapable or not in control, tends to make grown men and women deny social problems until they blow up in their faces. It's also, of course, a matter of ideology and how politicians rank priorities. In Jerusalem, unfortunately, welfare services and personal work for families take a back seat to other municipal work."

Despite the jarring conclusion of his work in the Jerusalem municipality, Eliezer felt great satisfaction from the time period during which he ran their Welfare Department. For the first time, he experienced the ability to lead social moves from a managerial position in a public system, a feeling he had been sorely missing in the ivory tower of academia.

"One of my greatest pleasures during all this time was being surrounded by my former students. They have guts, they feel for people,

and they want to change things. The missing ingredient seems to be leadership. Without that, they get depressed, demoralized, and crawl into themselves. I don't think social work will be exactly the same here after the 'Jerusalem experiment,' especially since social workers all over the country took note of what we did here. It was a real laboratory."

Eliezer was convinced that, in time, the mayor would also recognize the magnitude of the changes he made in the municipal Welfare Department. He also expected that some of the steps he took would have far-reaching national implications for social policy and the organization of welfare services. Indeed, at least one move made by Eliezer in the Jerusalem municipality was later adopted at the national level as well. As noted, Eliezer worked to transfer the distribution of financial support from the social workers to "eligibility officials" who were specially trained for this.

The success of the model in Jerusalem led to new employees being hired in all the welfare departments in the country, whose job was to distribute the financial benefits on a basis that did not depend on receiving other assistance, thus creating a separation between the social workers and those responsible for the distribution of funds. The next step in the revolution of the separation between the provision of funds and treatment, was the transfer of responsibility for the payment of income support fees from local authority employees to the central government.

Leading this move was Eliezer's colleague at the School of Social Work, Dr. Israel Katz, who served as Minister of Labor and Social Welfare from 1977-1981. During his tenure, the Income Maintenance Law was enacted in the Knesset, which transferred the responsibility for the payment of income support fees from the municipal welfare offices to the National Insurance Institute. Thus, an experimental

and initial move made by Eliezer in the Jerusalem municipality became, after about a decade, a national move that improved the work of all social workers in the country. Eliezer went on vacation for a few weeks before returning to university. He spent most of his vacation with his family, who had been somewhat neglected by him due to his intensive work in the municipality. A few days before he finished his job, Rivka told him that Ruti and Naomi, the two-and-a-half-year-old twins, cried and complained that their father barely came home to say good-night to them before bed. One night they even asked Rivka for a photo of Eliezer to tell him 'Good night' .... but despite his return to academia, Eliezer did not intend to seclude himself in the ivory tower. The social "bug" that had been implanted within him, soon brought him to new public and social action.

## Chapter Five

## Blessed with Children

Just two weeks after finishing his job as director of the Jerusalem municipality's Welfare Department, Eliezer set out on a new social mission. During one of his last days at the Jerusalem municipality, a man named Avraham Danino entered Eliezer's office and presented him with a vision - to establish an association of large families who will speak for themselves, without the mediation of professionals and politicians. It would be an association that would bring pressure on the powers-that-be to achieve rights and benefits for their families, and would give large families a status of respect in Israeli society.

Danino was a member of the Haifa City Council, a social worker by profession who supervised programs for children in need on behalf of the Ministry of Education. He was a member of a large family who immigrated to Israel from Morocco during the establishment of the state and was, himself, the father of a large family. When he despaired of political life, he sought another avenue for leading social change and thus conceived the idea for the new organization.

Eliezer was very impressed with Danino and with his vision. He, too, was exposed, through his research at the university and his work at the municipality, to the fact that large families should establish an organization. Eliezer thought that families should speak

for themselves, and he believed that when they do, people listen. He believed that all the social workers and all the statesmen would not be able to present the claims of large families better than the families would. When Danino entered his office and presented his vision to Eliezer, he felt the time was right for the vision to be fulfilled. "We are broadcasting on exactly the same wavelength," he later wrote.

On March 22, 1972, 7 Nissan 5732, the new organization called "Zahavi" (a Hebrew acronym for "Rights for Families Blessed with [many] Children") was founded in Haifa. Other public figures who were partners in the establishment of Zahavi were Rabbi Simcha HaCohen Kook, rabbi of the city of Rehovot, and Dr. Eugene Weiner, head of the Department of Sociology at the University of Haifa. At a press conference held by the organization's founders in Haifa, they explained that the purpose of the new organization was not to address problems of welfare and poverty, but to take care of the rights of *every* family with many children in Israel, including families with means, and that their intention was to promote legislative initiatives and tax benefits for the benefit of all large families. They called on every family with four or more children to join the organization, with a one-time registration fee of ten Israeli pounds (*lirot*). Half a year after the organization was founded, 650 families had already joined.

One of the struggles of its founders was already embedded in the name of the new organization. Eliezer and his friends in the management of Zahavi insisted on calling the families for which the organization was established "families blessed with children" and not "families with many children" as they were called until then. This decision stemmed from their perception of these families as a blessing to the State of Israel and not a social problem. The fact that its name, "Zahavi," means "my gold," sent a message that the children of Israel are its gold and its treasure.

At the time of the establishment of Zahavi, there were 96,000 large families in Israel. Although they made up only about ten percent of all families in the country, their children made up more than forty percent of all Israeli children. Zahavi leaders claimed that almost every second soldier in the IDF was from such a family, yet there was still a tendency to attribute to these families a negative image of the poverty-stricken.

In an interview with the Maariv newspaper about the movement's goals, Avraham Danino said: "If there is justification for a subsidy for factory production, why not give a subsidy for 'birth production' as well. If special rights are given to flower growers in Israel to grow and market flowers, why are there not rights for those who are growing human flowers? We want them to recognize the children's 'growers' just as they recognized the flower growers."

Eliezer greatly admired Danino. In a letter he wrote to his brother Yitz, he called him "one of the few contemporary Israeli pioneers," and explained: "Most people think the Zionist visionaries are all dead, but modern pioneering is not swamp-reclamation, and it's not living in a kibbutz, or even settling the Jordan Valley or the Shomron (Samarian) frontiers. I believe that today's pioneering involves the struggle for the soul of Israel, for the cultural survival of the different ethnic groups that have come here, and for the breaking-down of stereotypes and social classes that will one day boomerang on us all."

Zahavi was a social organization, not a protest organization. It sought to help families with children within the existing systems. Branches of the movement were soon established in Safed, Kiryat Shmona, Ashdod, Dimona, Hadera, Netanya and many other places. The establishment of the Jerusalem branch of Zahavi was initiated by Eliezer, and the person who actually ran the branch was Moshe Avital.

The activities of Zahavi's branches were held at the municipal level. The branch staff worked with local businesses to obtain discounts for large families, held discounted sales of bedding, towels and books, and distributed fruits and vegetables donated to the families. Yona Cohen, who was the treasurer of the Jerusalem branch of Zahavi, relates that it was important to Eliezer that the families pay a token amount for most of the products they received, so that they would not feel as if they were poor.

Other activities that took place at the Jerusalem branch were subsidized enrichment classes in English, mathematics and language, that were taught to students from large families. The teachers were new immigrants looking for work, so the project helped both immigrants and children. Another activity initiated by the Jerusalem branch was the organization of vacation day events for the parents of the families.

Some Zahavi branches opposed projects of direct assistance to families. Some Zahavi members believed that the organization's goal should be to obtain discounts and loans and not to distribute groceries that reinforced the families' image of themselves as welfare recipients. Eliezer, on the other hand, believed that the branches should also provide certain tangible services, if only to maintain direct contact with the families that were members of the organization.

Miriam Schlossberg, a friend of Rivka Jaffe's from childhood, had twins at her first birth. Three years later she and her husband had triplets -- three daughters. With the help of Eliezer and the members of Zahavi, Schlossberg created a group of parents of triplets to encourage support for each other. The group's meetings were held at Zahavi's Jerusalem branch. "Eliezer was all giving and kindness, without any personal gain," Schlossberg recalls. "He helped us, the parents of the triplets, wholeheartedly."

The support of government ministries to parents of triplets was given to families only a few months after the birth, and the families needed financial assistance until government support was received. Eliezer offered to lend each family, interest-free, a sum of money for their many needs in the first months after birth, until they would receive support money from the state. The parents-of-triplets group held regular meetings where they heard lectures on child rearing, education and medicine.

Not long after its establishment, Zahavi had already achieved quite a lot. Ten local authorities recognized the status of families with children in the area of property taxes and granted them discounts. In authorities in which property tax was paid according to the number of rooms, a family with four children received an exemption from taxes on one room. Families with five to seven children received a tax exemption on two rooms and families of eight or more children received a full tax exemption. In authorities in which property taxes were paid according to the size of the apartment, a family with four children received an exemption on thirty square meters, a family with five to seven children received an exemption on sixty square meters and a family with eight children or more received a full exemption. Some of the local branches of Zahavi succeeded in obtaining discounts for municipal summer camps, kindergartens and theater tickets.

The members of Zahavi made gains not only at the local level, but also at the national level. With the help of a lobby that was created in the Knesset, they achieved recognition of mothers of large families as working mothers eligible for added financial benefits, including

an extra six months of National Insurance Institute[4] payments and a semi-annual financial benefit from the National Insurance Institute. Going forward, another achievement was an amendment to the "National Water Law," according to which discounted water tariffs were granted to large families.

The greatest struggle of Zahavi, which began in 1974, was a struggle for the enactment of the "Law of Families Blessed with Many Children." The goal was to enact a law that would have all the rights and privileges of large families anchored in the Book of Israeli Statutes. The law would define large families as every family that has four or more children, up to the age of 21, including adopted children. The bill spoke of free education for children of large families, free admission or discounts to cultural institutions and events, the granting of preferential terms for mortgages and priority to public housing.

The suggested law also offered these families discounts on public transportation and electricity, on telephone and water payments, and one-time benefits like those given to new immigrants. It was also proposed to abolish the tax on the National Insurance Institute grant given to families. Another section of the bill proposed an annual income tax credit for any child over three children, as well as a negative income tax credit in case the breadwinner in such a family is not liable to income tax due to his low salary.

Members of Zahavi worked for many months to gather thirty thousand signatures from citizens who supported the draft of the bill. The signatures were presented to the President and Prime Minister and 52 Members of Knesset from various parties signed a

---

4   Israel's National Insurance Institute is parallel to America's Social Security.

petition supporting the law. The draft bill later received signatures from 66 MKs, including the support of the Prime Minister and the leader of the opposition faction, but in the end, the law, as drafted by Zahavi, never passed in the Knesset. However, some sections of the law were passed as independent laws, promoted by Zahavi, such as the "Free Education for High School Students Law" passed in 1979. Eliezer later claimed that the "Families Blessed with Many Children Law" was not passed in its entirety because none of the parties really cared to pass it, but were only thinking of how to use the law to enhance their political image.

One of the main problems of large families was housing. In the mid-1970s there were about twenty thousand large families living in difficult housing conditions. The 115,000 children of these families then constituted 12 percent of all Jewish children in Israel. Eliezer and his friends from Zahavi submitted a five-year plan to the government to solve the families' housing shortage in the country. They proposed to direct nine percent each year from the Department of Housing budget to building apartments for large families. Zahavi officials claimed that the harsh reality in the housing sector was adversely affecting the birth rate and causing a decrease in the number of large families in the country.

\*\*\*

On Yom Kippur, 5734, the sixth of October, 1973, the Yom Kippur War broke out.

Egyptian and Syrian forces launched a massive attack on Israel and managed to surprise the Israeli army in the early stages of the war and inflict heavy losses. The Jaffe family heard the sirens that shook Jerusalem, and they went down to the bomb shelter in the

basement of their apartment building together with their neighbors. Eliezer wrote to Yitz: "Four-year-old Ruti began crying and asked to take her guinea-pigs with her, and I calmed her down, saying I'd run up to check them every once in a while (and to get water and food, too).

"As the radio broadcasted code names of reserve units for call-up and I didn't hear mine, I went to volunteer at Shaare Zedek Hospital, now converted to a military hospital. For the next few days I worked with the social services department on special cases. One woman was brought to the hospital in hysterics – she had just seen her husband on Egyptian television, led captive from one of the strongholds that had fallen along the Bar Lev Line. I tried to comfort her by saying that she at least had proof he was alive and walking under his own steam. I finally got her home, helped her with the kids, and got a relative of hers to stay over for a while. She had five children in a two-and-a-half room flat in the Talpiot *shikunim* (housing development). They were from Iraq, poor as you can imagine. Two of her boys were in the army, G-d knows where. My heart really went out to her. This is Am Yisrael! Not supermen, but simple people trying to raise their children as best they can under difficult circumstances. Without them here, none of us would be here."

Several days later, difficult news reports began to arrive from the front. About 2600 soldiers fell in battle. Many of them were friends and acquaintances of Eliezer's. David Katz, a graduate of the Department of Sociology at the Hebrew University, who was an instructor at the School of Social Work, fell on the second day of the war as a reservist at the Ketubah post, one of the strongholds of the Bar Lev Line in Sinai. One of his daughters was in a class with Yael. "He was a modern *tzadik* (righteous person). I do not think he had an enemy in the world," Eliezer wrote of him.

Amos Miller, an economist who coordinated the budgets of the social ministries in the budget division of the Ministry of Finance, was killed by air gunfire on the southern front. Shortly before the war, he and Eliezer prepared a proposal for a joint research project. Chana, his wife, was Rivka's classmate at university. Sariel Birnbaum, the son of Deborah, who later was Naomi's teacher, was killed on the second day of the war in the containment battles in the Golan Heights. Moshe Danino, the son of Avraham Danino, founder and chairman of the Zahavi organization, was killed in Sinai in the ADF vehicle in which he was traveling.

When Eliezer went to comfort the Danino family in Haifa, Avraham repeated his custom of comparing children to flowers, and said to Eliezer: "We were very busy growing our own flowers and now we must help others to grow theirs." The mourning for those killed in the war was unbearable; there were so many. "Who can console?" Eliezer wrote to his brother. "Who has the right words? Who even understands?" About seven thousand soldiers were also wounded in the war. One of them was Yehoshafat Harel, Eliezer's and Rivka's friend who was wounded in the leg in the last days of the fighting. Eliezer assisted Yehoshafat by volunteering to drive him from his home in Jerusalem to Tel HaShomer Hospital for rehabilitation.

Eliezer joined in the public outrage that prevailed in Israel towards Prime Minister Golda Meir and Defense Minister Moshe Dayan. "We have never had a war like this, and people are frustrated and angry," he wrote. "Golda and Dayan should be ashamed to show their faces. We were caught so unprepared and off guard, it is pitiful. Even if Golda knew in advance, as she claims, and wanted to prevent a pre-emptive attack or angering the Americans, by what right did they sacrifice so many lives and families? I, for one, will never forgive them for what they allowed to happen, and from what

I hear, people are fed up with their leadership. If we had elections next week, Begin would be in with a breeze. Whoever heard of one party ruling for so many decades in a democratic country?"

A few days later, Eliezer was called up to reserve duty and sent to the southern sector together with other academics. Eliezer was drafted at a time when the IDF had already managed to block the Egyptian army, cross the Suez Canal and encircle the forces of the Third Army of the Egyptian army. The force that Eliezer joined crossed the canal and joined the forces that besieged the city of Suez.

Eliezer and his friends were instructed to help the officers raise the morale of the soldiers and to deliver lectures in their areas of expertise. "Jews are always ready to listen to lectures and to study even in the most difficult or strange situations," Eliezer wrote to his brother. "As 'older' men, all professors, we were seen by some of the young soldiers and officers as father figures, and I spent more than a few late nights comforting young officers who had seen their men killed in action, and listening to older, family men, deeply worried about how their wives were holding the family together, without help or even income. Who would fix the leak in the Friedman heater? Who would fix the hole in the children's bedroom window? Who would visit the wife about to give birth? This is the longest war Israel has fought and we're not built for long wars.

"The worst moment of all was one night near the little port of Adabiya, on the Gulf, south of Suez, when we were all suddenly assembled to hear a talk by the regimental doctor. Intelligence had heard that the Moroccan soldiers nearby were planning a gas attack. All of us were issued with gas masks and syringes and told how to counter the effects of gassing. It was horrible to hear, yet the doctor went on like he was teaching a cooking class, and I admired him for his calm.

"On another night, in a former Egyptian army base near Jebel Jenifa, we were all asleep with our clothes and boots on as ordered, when we were suddenly awakened at 3 A.M. and loaded aboard trucks. With lights off, the long convoy slithered out of the camp and deposited hundreds of us in the open desert several kilometers away. As we lay in the trenches, word went around that an enemy artillery or commando attack was expected, and since the camp was zeroed-in by the enemy, we had been evacuated. We waited all night, talking quietly in the dark. One poor soul was so frightened he insisted on sleeping in my trench since he was sure, 'nothing would happen' to me. After a while, you really do have to believe that nothing can happen to you. Otherwise, if you dwell on what can happen, you are lost. It's a 'war-zone mentality,' I guess. Anyhow, we were one bunch of happy guys when that sun finally came up on the desert. Maybe we were just lucky."

One day a delegation of American Jews came to express solidarity with the IDF soldiers at the front. Eliezer wrote to his brother Yitz that this visit raised his spirits but afterwards he also felt a sense of anger toward their visitors. "But it was a great feeling to see them, I must say. Nutty, but nice. Everybody was shaking hands and kibbitzing, the cameras clicking and everybody was speaking English. And then, just as suddenly as they came, they all got back on the bus… and drove off. And it was silent again. Only the birds, and the mango trees, and the Egyptians, and us, were left. We had been emotionally lifted up and then dropped with a thud. In two days, they would be on a plane back to the states with their pictures and their stories, and we were left with the mangoes and the Egyptians. Whose war was it, only ours? Did they think we're on a movie set? If you ever did a thing like that to me, Yitz, I'd disown you."

Despite the difficult war, when Eliezer encountered Egyptian

prisoners brought for interrogation, he felt no hatred for them. "I looked at those young Egyptian kids, straight into their eyes. Their hands were tied behind their backs. They were no older than your own son, Daniel, and very scared. These kids hadn't even finished high school, and they were already killing Jews with sophisticated anti-tank weapons and were handling SAM missiles. And we were killing them too. For how long, only G-d knows. It's so stupid and wasteful. I should have hated them, but I didn't."

In mid-November, about five weeks after the start of the war, Eliezer went on leave from his service at the front. He arrived in Jerusalem bearded, dirty and very tired. As he approached his home on Azza Road, he met Debbie, Yitz's oldest daughter, who had made aliya a year earlier to study social work at Hebrew University. "She gave me the biggest smile you can imagine," he wrote to Yitz, "and told me about what she and our other students are doing while the universities are closed, and about your letters to her, and about Mom. I just sat there and soaked it all up and it was good to be home again. When the twins saw me, they insisted I shave off my white beard. 'We want our father back the way he was,' they said. Well, I shaved off the beard easily enough, but I don't think I'll ever be quite exactly the way I was. People shouldn't ever take life for granted, or squabble over nonsense. We never know how much time we have, and we should use it and enjoy it as best we can."

In January, 1974, Eliezer went for another reserve period to the southern front. In a telegram to Rivka, he wrote: "We have a group of four lecturers and a driver, and I, imagine, am the squad commander ..." In another telegram he wrote: "It's not so nice but what can we do. I saw the building where Yehoshafat Harel was wounded and we will sleep in it tonight. It should have been a relatively protected headquarters, but in fact everything is so close that there is no such

place. I'm fine, and the soldiers are thirsty for talks, so it's not so terrible ... "

When the war ended, Eliezer returned to work at the School of Social Work and to his social activities within the management of Zahavi's national organization. In spite of the fact that during the war social problems were put on the sidelines, they of course did not disappear, and in some ways they increased. In October, 1975, Eliezer spoke at the conference of a United Jewish Appeal mission from America that took place in Jerusalem. He claimed that the ethnic gap in Israeli society was deepening and warned of an outbreak of riots on the background of social gaps. "When the security situation calms down a bit, then will come the eruption and we can already feel the agitation boiling beneath the surface."

Zahavi people did not hesitate to criticize the government's attitude to large families. In 1976, when the Ministry of Finance sought to decrease grants for children, Eliezer and Avraham Danino came out strongly against him. In an interview with Maariv, Eliezer said that the government had an agenda to present these families in a negative light, because it was not interested in large families, but did not have the courage to say so openly.

He even claimed that they were trying to give these families a negative image in order to be perceived by the public as parasites. As proof of this, he pointed to the fact that the only government representatives interviewed on the issue of large families were the Minister of Welfare and the Minister of Police, in order to give the families an image of poverty and crime. Eliezer and Avraham Danino accused the Ministry of Finance of defaming large families by publishing incorrect findings on the connection between receiving grants and dropping out of the labor market. "G-d forbid for the general public to be deceived by this distortion of the image of large

families, who only want to continue to exist with dignity, and not be supported by welfare."

A political upheaval took place in Israel in 1977. After almost thirty years of rule by the Labor Party, the people elected the Likud to power, led by Menachem Begin. Zahavi had high hopes for the new government. A high percentage of large families were from the Sephardic[5] public who identified with the Likud and supported it in the elections. In an article published in Maariv about two months after the election, Eliezer wrote: "Most of the Likud's support comes from the lower and middle classes and from the Sephardic electorate. Now that the Likud recognizes the need to reach this electorate, it may be in its power to give more than lip service to social issues. " Eliezer also hung hopes for social change on the Dash party, the centrist party headed by Yigael Yadin, who won fifteen seats in the election.

Dr. Israel Katz, a friend of Eliezer's from the School of Social Work, was one of the leaders of the Dash party and had drafted their social clauses. In an article that Eliezer published during the process of Dash's negotiations to join the government, Eliezer called for Katz to be appointed Minister of Social Welfare. He protested the fact that the negotiations between the Likud and Dash were focusing more on political issues than on welfare issues. "I would urge Dash to join

---

5   There are various terms used for Jews who came originally from Arab countries, including those who migrated to those countries from Spain and Portugal during the Inquisition, and including Jews who found themselves in other Arab countries, such as Yemen. They have been called "Sephardic," "Eastern," "Oriental," "Mizrahi" and "Edot Hamizrah." For the purposes of simplicity, we use the word "Sephardic" throughout, when relating to any of these groups.

the coalition and not get caught up in the border issue until serious negotiations with the Arabs begin," Eliezer wrote. "At the very least, in the long interim period, we can try to make peace with ourselves and finally approach work on social change and the ethnic split that threatens our existence from within." About two months later, Dash entered the government and, to Eliezer's delight, Minister Katz was appointed Minister of Welfare.

Following the intensification of the activities of Zahavi, the organizational burden increased, and the Zahavi staff asked the Ministry of Labor and Social Welfare for a grant that would allow them to employ a community worker. Ministry officials hesitated to approve the request because until then they had only supported the beneficiaries themselves and not the organizations that represented them, but in the end Minister Israel Katz decided to approve the grant.

However, a few months after the government was formed, Zahavi members were disappointed with its economic policy. The government severely narrowed subsidies and as a result, the price of basic foods and other items was raised, a reality that made it difficult for large families. In 1979 there was an economic deterioration in the financial situation of the country and inflation climbed to an unprecedented level and high prices became a regular phenomenon. The government decided that prices on essential items could be raised by fifty percent, and it became even more difficult for large families.

In December, 1979, the Zahavi movement staged a protest against the government's economic policy at Malchei Yisrael Square in Tel Aviv, with the participation of hundreds of parents and children of large families. The demonstrators protested the high price of living and the fact that the government was not advancing the passing of the "law for large families". They demanded compensation for the many price increases and also demanded linkage between the grants

to the families and the average wage in the economy. Eliezer said in a demonstration: "The government is harming children, who are the most important natural treasure we have."

A month later, the heads of Zahavi went out to fight for the increase in child benefits. At a press conference, they pointed out that between 1975 and 1979, the rate of child benefits decreased by a third compared to the salary increase. Eliezer claimed at the same event that 20 billion Israeli pounds had accumulated in the coffers of the National Insurance Institute as a result of the decreasing in grants and he warned against transferring the control of the money of the National Insurance Institute funds to the Ministry of Finance.

The struggle of the Zahavi people also led them to a direct confrontation with the mayor of Jerusalem, Teddy Kollek. In the local elections held in 1978, Eliezer and Avraham Danino called on families with children in Jerusalem to not vote for Kollek in the election. There were more than twenty thousand large families with close to 150,000 people and in spite of that, the Jerusalem municipality was among the few in the country that gave no benefits to those families.

Seven years after the establishment of Zahavi, the organization had twenty thousand families as members. Twenty branches of the organization had been established throughout the country, from Shlomi, Ma'alot and Safed in the north to Sderot and Dimona in the south. In 1977, the first branch of Zahavi was opened overseas, in Cleveland. It was established by Yitz and Miriam Jaffe, the brother and sister-in-law of Eliezer, and its main goal was to raise donations for the organization's branches in Israel.

Zahavi began to receive support from Jews in different countries who were interested and who learned about the problems of the large families in Israel. However, it was not easy to raise donations for Zahavi because the big donors preferred to donate to buildings

and hospitals rather than to an organization of citizens for social change. They preferred a building or sign that would commemorate their donation over intangible social activities. In 1976 Eliezer wrote a column in The Jerusalem Post, entitled "The Jewish Right to Reproduce." Sam Jacobson, a Jew from Nova Scotia, Canada, read the article and sent Eliezer a congratulatory letter with fifty dollars to Zahavi.

Three months later, Jacobson arrived in Jerusalem and asked to meet with Eliezer and Avraham Danino. After the two presented the organization's activities to him, Jacobson gave a large grant to Zahavi and conditioned it on the organization publishing weekly, in two major newspapers, ads praising families with many children. The ads benefited the public image of the large families.

"When I go to a Zahavi meeting, national or local, it's a pleasure to see all the ethnic groups there, Sephardi and Ashkenazi, and all the religious and political groupings," wrote Eliezer. "The major thing we all have in common is that each of us has at least four children. This Jewish-Israeli schizophrenia about large families is pathological. The chairman of the Knesset Finance Committee told me the other day that having large families is a great idea and terribly important for the country, but we should understand that we were going to have a hard time clothing, feeding and educating them because nobody in their right mind would raise a large family these days! Another Knesset member, a 'liberal' from the Labor Alignment party, asked: 'Why do you call yourselves families "blessed" with children? You should call yourselves families "cursed" with children.'

"With Jews like that, who needs the Fatah? According to Israeli demographers, by 2020 there will be a Moslem state here in Israel simply because the average Moslem mother in Israel gives birth to eight children. Besides, why shouldn't parents who like children be

able to exert the option to have them, and receive social supports to raise them in a Jewish State? I don't understand why we have to be like the goyim in everything, including zero population growth. For us, it's also a matter of physical and cultural survival as Jews.

"Last week I read a pseudo-sociological article in an American Jewish women's magazine claiming that all the recent talk about Jewish demography is actually a male plot to get Jewish women back into the kitchen, and cancel the gains of the Jewish women's liberation movement. How far-out can you get? I'm not against family planning, but I'll fight as hard as I can, too, for the other option, the option to plan to *have* a large family."

## Chapter Six

## A Family Man

The 1970s were Eliezer's peak years in academia and in social activism, but parallel with his public activities, these were also significant years for him and Rivka regarding their family. Rivka graduated with her Social Work degree in 1963, but did not work as a social worker for about thirteen years because she chose to devote her time to raising their four children.

As she was the one who spent many hours with the children, Rivka was the primary educator at home. She was the one who supervised the discipline, who set boundaries, studied with the children for exams, did homework with them and also sang them a lullaby at bedtime.

Eliezer devoted most of his day to work and to public activity. He went to the university -- or to city hall while he worked there -- early in the morning and returned in the evening. Even when he returned home, he would devote much of his time to writing or to checking students' work, so he would close himself up in his study. The main times he spent with his children were on Shabbat, during the *hagim* (holidays) and on vacations. Perhaps because he spent little time with his children in their daily routine, Eliezer allowed himself to be softer and more accepting than Rivka, who took upon herself the

burden of education and maintaining a framework. Eliezer's parenting was characterized not only by softness and acceptance, but also by a lot of fun, playfulness and humor. The light-hearted and childlike aspects of Eliezer's personality were expressed in his relationship with his children. Eliezer used to watch cartoons with them, that he loved as much as they did (later, he continued with this custom with his grandchildren as well), he would tell them jokes, laugh and fool around with them. He was discovered to have a special talent, which was guessing the end of thrillers and mystery films. "Pay attention to a certain line, to the clothing, to the angle of the film. It may have meaning later on."

When Yael's class played the game "The Dwarf and the Giant" (a game in which each child is a giant who has a dwarf - another child in the class -- who brings him surprises, without revealing his identity), Yael composed a poem for the girl who was her "giant" and in order for that girl to not recognize who sent it, Eliezer offered to call the girl's home, and to read the poem to her in a heavy American accent.

When Eliezer and Rivka decided to buy a new car, he brought home a fan of colors and asked the children to choose their favorite color for the new car. The children pointed to a bright blue color, like the color of a toothbrush they liked, and Eliezer had the car painted in the requested unconventional color that could be seen from a distance.

The children of the Jaffe family remember the small gifts their father would bring with him from his travels in Israel or when he lectured abroad. One of the most memorable was a lost turtle he found on his way home. In general, Eliezer loved pets. Despite Rivka's initial reservation about raising animals at home, he encouraged the children to raise hamsters, guinea pigs, rabbits and also a dog

named Skippy, who owed her life to him after he calmly rescued her from drowning in the Yarkon River.

In the living room of the family home was an unusual souvenir cabinet where Eliezer placed fossils, a collection of framed spiders, sea shells and other mementoes. Josh Zucker, the grandson of the late Yitzhak (Yitz), Eliezer's brother, shared that throughout his childhood, and especially regarding the cabinet in question, he believed that Saba Eliezer was none other than Indiana Jones.

Noy Jaffe, his granddaughter, relates, "I remember we would walk into an apartment on Azza Road and smell the pungent smell of old wood and good memories. I especially remember the old wooden cabinet in the living room in which Saba collected all the souvenirs he and Savta had bought around the world -- the frog that would croak as you passed a wooden rod over its back, stuffed birds, and the huge collection of pipes (which I only later realized Saba would occasionally smoke, when it was more in fashion). Beneath all the shelves of souvenirs was our favorite part of the cabinet - piles of tapes with cartoons.

"I remember how the grandchildren would sit on the pull-out couch, waiting our turn to see who would get to sit on it and watch Bugs Bunny. How we would laugh and act out scenes from the tapes! Even years later, when the TV was replaced and the VCR left our world - the white sofa remained, a place of rest when we came to visit Grandpa."

Eliezer's playfulness was also reflected in the creative ideas he gave to Rivka. One day he suggested that instead of singing lullabies to the children every night before bed, she should record herself singing and play the recording in the bedroom for them. Rivka adopted the idea and used the extra time for housework. The ploy was revealed when one night, together with the lullabies that emerged

from the recording, Naomi and Ruti heard their mother talking on the phone and got out of their beds to figure out what was going on.

A similar story involved a TV series that the girls loved to watch, which aired late at night. Rivka and Eli conditioned the viewing of the show on the girls sleeping in the afternoon, and also limited their viewing time in general. One day, the twins were amazed to hear the tune of their favorite show playing in the living room in the early afternoon. When they hurried to the living room, they found that the television was off and next to them their father was standing and laughing, with the recording device in his hand. The night before, Eliezer had recorded the opening of the show to kid his little daughters.

At the family Shabbat meals, Rivka's centrality to the children's education was evident. Rivka, who came from a family of "Yekka" (German) descent, encouraged the singing of Shabbat *z'mirot* (songs) as was customary in her home, and she used to quote her father, Chaim Gershon, who was very meticulous about singing them all, and claimed that it should be done "so that no *z'mira* would be offended." Eliezer also loved to sing. Every Shabbat, Eliezer, Rivka and the four children would sing the familiar *piyutim*: "Tzur Mishlo," "Ya Ribon" and "Yedid Nefesh," along with songs from Rivka's parents' home, such as "Halleluyah" and "Sim Shalom," which they would perform as a canon, in two or three voices, with their voices overlapping. One of the songs that Eliezer especially loved was "Hamalach Hagoel" ("The Savior Angel"). This song would fill him with contentment, especially when it was later sung by his grandchildren.

On Shabbat mornings, Eliezer would hide candies that he bought in the shuk within his *tallit* (prayer shawl), and give them out generously to all the children in the shul. Even without candies, many children from his family and from other families were drawn to his

warm, glowing personality and felt that he had a sincere interest in them and in their world.

Rivka, who put a lot into enriching the knowledge of their children, was adamant, together with her daughter Yael, that at every meal there should be a *d'var Torah* (short Torah lesson) on *Parshat Hashavua* (the portion of the week). Eliezer and Rivka enjoyed talking to the children about their daily lives, and shared with the children value dilemmas that they encountered in the course of the past week. More than once, after the meal, Eliezer would sit by the feet of the children's beds and invent imaginative stories.

In his conversations with his children, Eliezer was a father who empowered them. He encouraged them to invest in their studies, to aim high and to dream big dreams, and he gave the message that they were capable of being high achievers. Rivka was the one who closely followed their achievements in school and who pushed them to spend time on their studies. Eliezer was the one who gave the inspiration and set the way, but were it not for the daily involvement of Rivka, the children would probably not have been able to implement his vision.

Unlike many immigrants who came to Israel from the United States, who retained their mother tongues and attempted also to instill them in their children who were born in Israel, Eliezer left his English behind. As one who insisted on teaching in Hebrew even in his first years in the country, he also insisted on Hebrew being the language of their home and did not try to push English on his children. At the same time, Eliezer did not totally distance himself from the American culture in which he had grown up. This manifested itself in certain dishes that he enjoyed, like cereal and ketchup (not together). He also loved to listen to country music, and he used English expressions of affection.

Rivka dedicated her time to raising the children for almost thirteen years. She worked only part time in research in the Department of Social Medicine (*Mahlaka l'Refua Hevratit*) in Hadassah Hospital. One of her projects was tracking chronically ill patients and another was conducting a community survey in the Kiryat HaYovel neighborhood. Rivka also dedicated significant time to volunteer work. She helped out large families -- mostly families who had twins or triplets -- advised families on childcare and on how to run a home, how to be in contact with various offices, how to reach out to various organizations or initiatives that could be helpful, and on how to obtain their legal rights.

She also volunteered in Zahavi, the organization of which Eliezer was a co-founder, and she organized groups of families with special issues in order to help them help each other and to receive benefits to which they were entitled. One of the struggles she helped lead was to subsidize special food for celiac babies.

In 1974, 5735, Eliezer took a sabbatical for a year and the Jaffe family went to live in Cleveland. Together with the time he spent writing and working in research, Eliezer was active in creating a local branch of supporters of Zahavi. He also received requests from Israel's Ministry of Foreign Affairs, and from Israeli consulates, to give lectures, but he could not respond to all of them.

One of the lectures that he gave on social problems in Israel was at the annual conference of the United Jewish Appeal that took place in New York. At the conference, whose title was, "We Are One People," Golda Meir, who had resigned from being Prime Minister a few months earlier, also spoke.

Rivka took advantage of the sabbatical in Cleveland to attend courses at the local College of Jewish Studies. She took courses in swimming and was involved in activities of the local Jewish community.

In the wake of an article that appeared in Maariv, Rivka also got involved in raising funds for the resuscitation unit of Rambam Hospital in Haifa. She invited Dr. Shimon Burstein, the head of the department, to Cleveland, and he gave a lecture before seventy members of the Jewish community who then donated to the department. Those present promised Rivka and Dr. Burstein that the money they collected at community events would be sent to buy equipment that was needed.

Uri started sixth grade during the sabbatical year, Yael was in fourth grade, and the five-year-old twins were in kindergarten. The family rented a spacious three-story house within easy walking distance of the home of Arthur-Yitz, Alvin, and Jack and the home of Sarah, Eliezer's mother. Alice, Eliezer's older sister, lived with her family in Cincinnati, in southwest Ohio.

The Israeli Jaffe children quickly connected to the rest of their local family and adapted nicely within the educational systems, but they did not forget for one moment that they were Israelis. One day, Yael came back from school and told Eliezer that she did not feel comfortable singing the U.S. national anthem every morning in her classroom, because this is not her country. Eliezer understood what Yael felt in her heart.

A few days later he went to school with Yael for a conversation with the class teacher and told her that Yael had a request. Yael asked the teacher that while the students sang the US anthem, she would quietly sing "Hatikva." The teacher agreed, and from that day on, so it was.

Eliezer and Rivka were impressed by the many donations that the Cleveland Jewish community collected for Israel, but they were also critical about life in the Diaspora. Rivka wrote a letter to her mother at the end of the High Holidays, during which time a large amount

of money was raised for the State of Israel. Among other things, she wrote, "With all the beauty of these donations, it is easy for them to give, because then they feel free to not make aliya, and feel that they are giving a lot of aid to Israel, but they don't really know or feel the situation in Israel and they don't have an emotional connection to what is happening there."

Rivka told her mother that on Tu B'Shvat the Israelis in Cleveland had a party. "We were 30 Israeli couples. We ate fruits of Israel and sang songs, that we projected on a wall, about planting and about trees. Songs from different time periods, from the distant past and more recent. There was something in the singing that drew us closer together and we can only hope that all those singing will return to Israel in the near future – some of them already concluded their studies and remained here to make a bit of money – and that they will not be tempted to remain in the land of abundance."

The Jaffe's spent the Pesach (Passover) holiday with the family at Yitz's home, together with all of Eliezer's siblings and their children. "We are already very excited about the great event, and the children are very enthusiastic," Rivka wrote to her mother a few days before the holiday. "We'll sleep over there, with everyone else, including the cousins from Cincinnati, since it is dangerous to walk around here at night, especially since recently there have been many instances of assault and attempted robberies, and it's about a forty-minute walk home. We'll stay there for the second seder also, as Grandma Sarah requested, and on Friday we'll return home."

Two weeks after Pesach, Rivka told her parents about an argument she had with the children's school principal, regarding the fact that the school did not note in any way Yom Hashoah v'HaGevurah ("Holocaust and Heroism Day," sometimes also known as "Holocaust Memorial Day") that falls on the 27th of the Hebrew month of

Nissan [in the spring]. "I asked for a clarification and he of course had nothing to answer. He said that he thought that the 10$^{th}$ day of Tevet [that fell a few months earlier] was the Yom HaShoah that was marked internationally.

I suggested that he add a ceremony marking Yom HaShoah into the curriculum and he said that perhaps I'm right and he'll think about it. I told him that we have enough "spies" in the school who can let me know if next year they will relate to it or not [even though we will no longer be there]. Rivka promised the principal that with her return to Israel, she would try to obtain materials on Yom HaShoah from the Ministry of Education and she would send them to the school in Cleveland before the next Yom HaShoah.

Yom Ha'atzmaut (Israeli Independence Day) also presented Rivka with a challenge. Within the Jewish community of Cleveland there was tension between the Israelis who were not Orthodox and the local Orthodox community. Before the Yom Ha'atzmaut party, the Israelis prepared a festive meal in "The Hebrew Youth House" (*Beit Hanoar Ha'Ivri*), but one of the Orthodox women was concerned that the food was not kosher and she announced this to all the members of the local Bnei Akiva branch.

The day before Yom Ha'atzmaut, the heads of the Bnei Akiva branch told their members that it was forbidden for them to eat at the party, and the non-Orthodox Israelis were insulted. Rivka heard about the incident. With the help of an Orthodox Israeli friend, she recruited a local rabbi who checked out the food that was prepared for the party, and he confirmed that the food was kosher. "All's well that ends well, everything went smoothly, but with unnecessary hatred," Rivka wrote to her parents.

"In the argument, I claimed that the attitude of the Orthodox here was in danger of widening the gap between the two communities.

Rather than volunteering themselves and explaining to the volunteers, who generally are not Orthodox, regarding how to prepare the food in a halachic fashion, [they acted in a way] that caused a bitter argument between us." In the end Rivka succeeded in organizing five Orthodox women who agreed to help the people of the "Hebrew Youth House" prepare the food for similar public events that would take place in the future. She also arranged for one of the rabbis to oversee the kashrut of the food in order to prevent tensions.

Even from his place of residence in Cleveland, Eliezer continued to monitor social problems in Israel and worked from afar to find solutions. Among other things, he corresponded with the Minister of Welfare at the time, Michael Hazani of the National Religious Party, and offered him various proposals for dealing with the welfare problems that he had to deal with. In a letter written by Minister Hazani to Eliezer in April, 1975, he thanked him for his suggestions and for the professional materials he sent him. Hazani even wrote to Eliezer that he agreed with him on promoting the idea of negative income tax as a guaranteed financial benefit to disadvantaged populations.

"I'm making real strides in the advancing of this issue," wrote Hazani, and he signed his letter, "I was especially happy for your opinion on the need for a specific office that would deal with human issues." But Hazani did not merit to meet Eliezer. He died suddenly two months later, before Eliezer returned to Israel.

In August, 1975, the Jaffe family returned home to Jerusalem. A new school year began, and the twins Naomi and Ruti entered first grade and for the first time were separated into two parallel classes. Eliezer and Rivka chose separation because they wanted to give each twin the opportunity to build an independent and separate identity for herself, each in her own class.

Fear of the first day of school was not just that the twins had been accustomed to being with each other since birth. Rivka also had a hard time accepting the separation of the girls. In the end, September 1st started with a smile. On their way to school, holding a hand of each twin, Rivka stumbled and slipped on the sidewalk. The girls, who were tense and excited for what would be happening that day, found an opportunity to release a bit of the tension and laugh. The shared laughter was burned into their consciousness of the first day of first grade. Later in the morning, they were already laughing less. Rivka brought each of the twins to her class and peeked in at them intermittently through a tall window in the classroom hallway.

A few months after the twins started school, Rivka went back to work, after many years that she had devoted to raising the children. She began working as a social worker at MATAV, an association for care and welfare services. The association, which was founded in the late 1950s and is still active today, provides nursing services for the elderly in their homes, manages day centers for the elderly and advises senior living homes and sheltered housing. When Rivka began working at MATAV she was a counselor-advisor and in the course of the years progressed in her positions.

She was responsible for the training of home-based caregivers, for the organizing of advanced education programs, became a member of the professional committees of MATAV and fourteen years later was appointed the director of the Jerusalem branch of MATAV, that included 450 caregivers and a staff of eleven social workers.

A good portion of Rivka's work was dedicated to the guidance of home caregivers who were taking care of the elderly. Rivka wanted the caregivers to respect the elderly person, to appreciate him as a person with a past and with an individual personality and not to relate to him only as one being cared for. She told the caregivers to

place next to the bed of the elderly person photos from the time of his childhood, his youth, and family celebrations, so the caregivers will know him as a person who was active and independent and not just as one who is dependent on others, as he is now. Rivka invited a family member of hers to train the caregivers on how to serve food to their patients in a way that is aesthetic, dignified and pleasant.

In order to help the caregivers identify with the elderly patient, she carried out an exercise during the caregivers' training. She asked one of the caregivers to put on glasses whose lenses were smeared with Vaseline, tuck cotton balls in her ears and to then go and place a cup of coffee on a table at the end of the room. The caregiver, who could not hear well and or see well, because of the limitations placed on her eyes and ears, had difficulty, as expected, in the task, and thus felt, in the flesh, some of the difficulties of the elderly that she would be looking after.

Eliezer went back to teaching at the School of Social Work and continued his social activism in various ways. In the middle of the 1970s he was, among other things, a member of the Committee for Social Services in the Jerusalem municipality, and a member of the committee that the Minister of Labor had founded whose mandate was to set the criteria, for those who had been disabled in work accidents, to receive cars.

In December, 1975, a conference took place in Jerusalem for the alumni of Yeshiva University of New York. At the conference's conclusion, prizes were awarded to three alumni who had made aliya to Israel and who excelled in their public activity. One of the recipients of the award was Eliezer, who received it in recognition of his work in the area of social activity.

## Chapter Seven

## "The One You Have Loved, Yitzhak"

In February, 1977, Eliezer was a guest writer in a special section of the Haaretz newspaper, which each week gave a peek into the daily life of one person with an interesting agenda. Under the heading "The Need for Action and the Love of Research," Eliezer described what he did that week. From the diary he wrote, one can learn quite a bit about his intense lifestyle and the challenging way in which he chose to combine his research and his work at the university, his extensive social activity, and his family life.

"Thursday: A very important day for me. Discussion in the school's admissions committee on my research proposal to accept students who are 't'unei tipuah' - from "disadvantaged"[6] families - who will be 20% of the next class in the School for Social Work, in

---

[6] The word "disadvantaged" is in quotes, as there is no precise translation of "t'unei tipuah." The literal translation is "those in need of cultivation and educational promotion" and it was usually used in the educational context, not in the economic context, though these two issues often overlapped, in a vicious cycle, as children who grew up in socially and culturally deprived environments/communities usually studied in schools that were less advanced academically.

1977, and have a plan that second and third year students connect with them, to help them cope with their studies, without lowering the level of education and requirements ... It is not right to have a situation in which only the score of the screening tests determines who will succeed in social work."

He went to the editorial offices of the Jerusalem Post. "I have submitted an article in which I demand that the federations of the Jewish communities in the United States take responsibility for providing assistance and following up on 'their' immigrants. The article was accepted for publication. The federations are embarrassed regarding everything involving the promoting of aliya and think that the UJA will save us. They take pride in 'Operation Entebbe' and at the same time they relate to our emissaries as if they are a foreign factor. In the afternoon, had a meeting with the Director of Special Projects of the National Insurance Institute.

"The Jerusalem branch of the Zahavi movement has submitted a proposal to establish a 'bank' for children's furniture, a store where members of the movement can buy and donate used furniture for children at token prices, retirees will renovate the furniture, we will collect it from donors in our car - a beautiful project. This would not be a general welfare initiative, but only for large families.

"The discussion was sympathetic and constructive; they are considering a serious grant, understand the issue and are a pleasure to work with. I wish all the offices behaved like the National Insurance Institute. Usually they want the volunteering, but not the volunteers. Then back home to the kids - four, including cute twins, and the wife. In the evening: Lecture on social problems in Israel before people from abroad who have come to dedicate a year of national service to Israel, that takes place in Ma'ale Hahamisha. They are good guys. Some will come back to us when they have acquired

various professions. Do we really want them? It's not simple.

"Friday: Shabbat is coming. Had a conversation with the head of the School of Social Work. Had to do with Admissions Committee issues (I am the chairman), and planning my teaching for next year. How am I to combine my need to be involved actively in bringing about changes in services and policies, with my love of research and teaching? It's difficult to teach students about what exists at the moment, and about the need for change, without being a personal role model and without really enjoying the work. Others succeed in disengaging, they compartmentalize. It's hard for me, but there's a price. In the evening, I'll be going to synagogue, enjoying the warmth of friends and family, I'll relax reading the newspapers and everything else that comes with Shabbat.

"Shabbat: The children climb all over our beds, waking us up with no mercy, to get to synagogue. The rabbi gives a talk aimed at both the bar mitzva boy and the adults, an excellent lecture, very knowledgeable. Kiddush, guests, family singing. Ruti, seven, is concerned that because a neighbor passed away this week, maybe we should move to another home to escape death. 11-year-old Yael has been getting closer to me since the father of her friend, who is also a family friend, was killed in a car accident. Rivka and I talk to them about death, about how nothing lives forever. It's not easy, and hard to know how much they understand. The subject is no longer abstract for them. That's how you grow up in this country, but in my opinion, it's too fast.

"The older kids of the Bnei Akiva branch in [the neighborhood of] Bayit Vegan asked to see my slides on poor neighborhoods in Jerusalem. It was Saturday evening and the hall was filled with young people who were listening, watching, reacting, and want to help. This increased consciousness is a natural response. I wonder; why

do they know so little about their neighbors in the asbestos huts and in the poor Katamonim neighborhood?

"Sunday: In the morning I lecture before third year students about "Welfare Services for the Child and the Family." They are excellent students, most of them women, getting ready for graduation and preparing for hard work in the profession. I wonder, how many will remain in the profession after five years? Are we giving them good tools, good skills? 845 applied this year for the School of Social Work but there is only room for 120. There are about 300 university graduates in social work each year, only 2,500 nationwide. How will this small army carry out its missions?

"Afternoon: I have reserve duty, almost one day a week, like clockwork. This time it is lectures for a tank commanders' course, 'somewhere' in Israel. They ask good questions about Israel's social policies, the Black Panthers, etc. There is a tendency to demand that others change social situations. I try to explain that the responsibility lies with all of us, including with tank commanders. Everyone must find a place where he can take action -- as a soldier with his soldiers and as a civilian with his children, and with himself -- at every opportunity. The base commander attends my lecture together with his soldiers, which a good sign. Here they care about 'internal problems'.

"It is a pleasure to see these young men. God bless them. I'm proud of them. In a few years, my Uri will be sitting among them. This little one is growing up so quickly. It's too late at night for these thoughts. I arrive home and enter quietly, as the kids are sleeping.

"Monday: Early in the morning my lecture is "Introduction to Sociology and Anthropology" for first year students. Today the topic is "Bureaucracy and Institutions." There are 120 students in the class. I give examples. "Societies receive and create the institutions they

deserve." So it is with us. I give out a questionnaire on young people's expectations regarding childbirth, relative to the size of their parents' families. An interesting final paper of third year students. It's a good questionnaire. I am already curious about the results and the data. In the afternoon I have reception hours, and I spend time on scientific writing and reading until late. I continue this at home, in the evening, with a short 'good night' break for the children, and to listen to the news, and then return to writing.

"Tuesday: Had a conversation with a new immigrant, a rabbi from the United States, about options for various volunteer jobs in Jerusalem. He's very interested in Zahavi. A group of students from the Evelina de Rothschild School are in the office, requesting information on the work of the Ministry of Welfare and welfare policy in Israel. *Kol hakavod* ("Well done!") to their teacher! This is a beautiful and practical job for children. Avraham Danino, chairman of Zahavi, came from Haifa to meet with a Swiss philanthropist who wants to establish a fund, through Zahavi, to encourage children of large families to return to school. Avraham's enthusiasm is really contagious.

"I really appreciate him. His son fell in the Yom Kippur War and he 'adopts' all the sons of Israel. I hope he continues to have strength. I spent the afternoon sitting at the home of District Judge Felix Landau, chairman of the Public Association for the Advancement of Youth in Jerusalem. Mickey, the community worker, and I suggest a number of issues for the care of the lost youth. The judge is aware and interested in the topic, and worried. He very much wants to improve services for them. He lives in the real world and not just in an ivory tower. He is prepared to put the Jerusalem municipality into action and there's a lot to do.

"Wednesday: Teaching at Bar Ilan University. At the gate I meet and drive my graduate students to a meeting at the office of

a Tel Aviv architect who plans services for the population in the Neve Eli'ezer neighborhood and Kfar Shalem. The students are designing a welfare service system for the neighborhood, under my supervision, as a practicum in social work. They review many beautiful maps, but one can see the gap between the physical planning and between the needs of the families in the field.

Who should adapt to whom? The maps to the residents or the residents to the maps? Where is the voice of the residents in the planning? Does a luxurious fountain in a dull grey neighborhood serve the needs of the fountain donor from abroad, or the locals?

"This piazza with its fountain will be a huge pile of rubbish in a few years, and what a shame that will be. It would be wiser to build a community center there. Perhaps my students and their work can impact the decision?

"In the afternoon, I corresponded with the head of the Personnel Division of the IDF and with the Minister of Defense, asking them to increase the number of candidates for the academic army program (*atuda*) in social work.[7] It is important to ensure professional work for 'Service Conditions' IDF officers, who are assigned to care for soldiers' well-being.[8] We are ready to accept them for studies if they meet the admission requirements, but the pool of candidates must be increased. We need to help the IDF understand the importance of the issue and move forward in the matter. Rivka calls. It's late again,

---

7   "Atuda" is a program in which students attend university before they are drafted, acquire a profession that is needed in the army, and commit to serving a number of years in that profession, as career officers, beyond the mandatory period.

8   These officers do work similar to that of social workers in the army.

and the children are waiting for a 'good night' from me."

On the morning of Rosh Chodesh Cheshvan, 5739, the first of November, 1978, the phone rang in the home of the Jaffe family. Rivka was not at home. She was taking the twins to school. Eliezer picked up the phone and was surprised to hear the voice of Minda, wife of his younger brother Jack. He knew that the hour in Cleveland was 2A.M. "I wondered why Minda was calling so late. 'Something has happened here,' said Minda." Eliezer thought about his elderly Mom. "Is Mom okay?" he asked, anxiously. "Yes, Mom is fine, but there was a robbery at the shop and Yitz was shot and killed."

Minda said, "Yitz was in the shop late last night, Eli. He was expecting a truck delivery. The driver called from the road to say that he had some mechanical problems with the truck and would be arriving late. Yitz said he would wait until 6 P.M. and then he'd have to let the workers go home and close up the shop until the next day. At six, the workers left and they expected that he would too.

"But while Yitz was locking up, the driver pulled in with the truck. Yitz knew that the load was expected in New York the next day, and since the driver was tired, he told him to rest while he loaded the truck himself. The driver went to sleep with the motor running so he could keep the cab heated. He never heard a thing until Alvin pounded on the locked door of the cab to wake him up.

"Yitz had been weighing the bales and then loading them into the trailer with the fork lift. Somebody must have come in off the street onto the loading dock. The overhead door was open because the cab of the trailer stuck out into the street. Somebody shot him and took his wallet and went through his pockets and ran away. Nobody saw him. Yitz had called Miriam to say he'd be late, but when she called him again at 7:30 P.M., no one answered, and she got worried. She called Alvin and he went down there with Arlene. They found Yitz

lying on the loading dock. Alvin ran out to the street to see if anyone was there, and banged on the cab of the trailer, and the driver woke up. He never heard a thing."

Eli was stunned by the terrible news. He had a deep and meaningful emotional connection with his older brother that spanned decades, even though the two were separated by continents and seas. Only a few months earlier, Yitz had purchased an apartment in the same Jerusalem building on Azza Road where the Jaffe family lived. In a letter to Eliezer, he wrote that he really planned to sell the shop one day and immigrate to Israel. "The idea of aliya has become less abstract," he wrote to his brother, but the killer's shots destroyed his plans.

Yitz's funeral was held on Wednesday in the sanctuary of Taylor Road Synagogue in Cleveland, where Yitz had been the president for four years. There had been very little time within which to inform people about the time or place of the service, but they all came. From all walks of life, from all segments of the community, they came. No, they did not just come. They were pulled, pulled by their heartstrings. Some came because they loved him. Others came because they admired him. But all came because they respected him. They came to pay their final tribute to Arthur Jaffe, who was snatched so prematurely from the world of the living, out of their profound affection and regard for him.

Rabbi Louis Engelberg spoke about the many types of roles that Yitz had filled in his life - president of the religious Zionist group Bar Ilan, head of the Rabbinical Committee of the Federation of the Jewish Community, a member of the College of Jewish Studies, head of the finance committee of Beit Hillel at Case Western Reserve University and more. He noted the exceptional hospitality in the home of Miriam and Arthur Jaffe, and spoke about Yitz's wisdom, courtesy and generosity. "He was a faithful and observant Jew, a truly

noble and sensitive soul, a very warm, open-hearted, popular man, with two feet on the ground."

Eliezer hurried to fly to Cleveland. He wasn't in time to attend the funeral of his beloved brother but arrived for the *shiva* [seven days of mourning]. Debby Zucker, Yitz's eldest daughter, remembers that towards the end of the shiva, Eliezer suggested to her and to the rest of the family to not make significant changes in their lives in the near future. "The most important thing is that you return to your routines now," he told them. "Keep the changes for later."

Eliezer returned to the United States several months later to see his mother and Miriam, Yitz's widow, and to help his grieving family as much as he could. In a letter he wrote to his dead brother seven months after his murder, he described the feelings of the family members.

"It's hard on everyone, of course, your being so cruelly yanked out of our lives, but each of us has to make peace with it. Mom is having the hardest time of all, because, whether you knew it or not, she was probably closest to you. And Alice, too, even though she's our older sister, has come to face the awful and fearful understanding that we are fragile, mortal beings, our very lives hanging on chance occurrences, fate, or G-d's Will, whichever you wish. She is fearful of what else may happen to us and to her loved ones, and cannot reconcile your death with your abundant good deeds."

Later Eliezer wrote, "One of the hardest things we had to do was to sell the shop. Not because of the mundane and often difficult negotiations or even the loss of income, but because the shop was a great part of you and of all the years of hard work and emotional investment which you put into it. And because it really was a visible symbol of our best memories of Pa, and of you, and of our own childhood days when Pa had us pitch in and learn what it meant to pull our weight. On the day before we handed over the building,

Alvin, Moe, Miriam and Jack, and cousins Rosina and Howard and some of the kids, went down to the shop and cleared out your office, bidding goodbye to it and to a part of you and Pa, for the last time.

"When I was in Cleveland two months ago, on the way to Miriam's house from the airport, I recalled the many times you had come from work to pick me up, stopping off at the shop to show me how things were going there, before taking me on to Mom's house. I wasn't prepared to break that tradition yet, to have anyone else pick me up, so I rented a car from Avis for the drive to Miriam's house. You wouldn't have approved of that, I know. A waste of money, to be sure.

"On the way downtown, I instinctively made a right turn on Carnegie Avenue at 65th Street. The car glided toward the shop as if pulled by some compelling force, and parked in front of those huge overhead doors by the loading dock. I sat there for nearly an hour, just recollecting and getting it out of my system."

Before returning to Israel, Eliezer went to his brother's grave in the Jewish cemetery on Aurora Road outside of Cleveland, and placed a small stone on it. He looked at the blue sky and recalled Yitz's first visit to Jerusalem, shortly after the Six Day War. "Out of your fifty years, you only spent fifty days in the Promised Land," he wrote of his brother. "One day for every year. Indeed, you were a true Zionist, and not just a fan of Zionism. It is a pity that you are now in exile on foreign land, so far from home. How meaningless to Jews are the names: Lansing, Cleveland, Aurora."

Eliezer was aware of the fact that, for most Jews in the United States, aliya to Israel was irrelevant, but he believed, and knew that Yitz also believed, that the only place for Jews to live at this time, and especially for religious Jews, was the State of Israel. He thought with irony about how Yitz worried for so many years about Eliezer's

safety and his family's safety in Israel, and now, he, Eliezer, is forced to mourn his brother who was murdered in the U.S., for no reason. He knew that if Yitz had immigrated to Israel, like him, in the early years of the State, he might have been killed in one of the wars in Israel but Eliezer believed that Jews should live and raise their children here, and also end their lives here, in Eretz Yisrael, and not on foreign land.

After Yitz's murder, Eliezer wrote in a letter, "I am bitter, as you can see. I'm bitter, Yitz, that we lived apart all these years, sustained mostly by letters, phone calls and telegrams, and long-planned, but quick-ending visits to each other. I'm bitter because our children couldn't grow up together, and especially because your talents and ingenuity were not used for us Jews here in Israel. I'm bitter more than anything else, because for nearly twenty years I have missed enjoying your company and for knowing now that there are no more letters, and no more long talks or visits, and no more time together.

"But bitterness and mourning have the quality of turning people to introspection and taking stock, and pulling long-lost memories out of the storerooms of our brain. Memories of good times lost make me sad, but I feel better for having remembered, nevertheless.

"We had a lot of good times together and the pain of losing loved ones is evidence of just how good and deep those relationships were. The more you love somebody, the more you're hurt when it's over. But the fact that I have those good memories to draw on, is comforting to me. 'Better to have loved and lost, than not to have loved at all'?

"My perspective on religion, by the way, has changed somewhat since your death. Mom's life has been shattered by the inconceivable injustice done her. She feels that the unwritten contract between her and G-d has been broken. She kept her part of the bargain and

raised her children to be decent Jews; G-d-fearing people, who never harmed anybody. G-d was supposed to protect them. And then, on the eve of Rosh Hodesh, some maniac shoots you down. She can't figure it out, no one can. She can't bring herself to blame G-d and she is inconsolable.

"I could never accept the fundamentalist view. I've seen too much circumstance in human affairs, good and bad. You were one of the few people who knew that I took religion with a grain of salt. You even chided me about it on several occasions and were troubled by it. For me, Judaism and ritual is the essence of a way of life, not a guarantee of life. It's what helps us define ourselves as Jews and gives us a rich family life, and meaning to life. It would be irrelevant to make G-d take the blame for your death. I suppose that the real miracle in life is that G-d keeps us alive as long as He does.

"We had other blessings too: we had you for 51 years, our parents were spared form the Holocaust, we had children, all healthy, and we were able to raise them in the way we wanted. We inherited a Jewish identity and belonging which gave our lives meaning. Our marriages stayed together. For all that, I am grateful. I think you would be the last person who would want us to respond to tragedy in life with impregnable bitterness and resentment; it wouldn't be in keeping with your personality or your legacy to us.

"But I must admit that I have lost much of the good cheer and sense of belonging and involvement that the synagogue and prayer, and especially communal singing, once filled me with. After you died, Yitz, I find myself sitting in the synagogue on Shabbat, singing less, and thinking and listening more to the tunes of the others in the congregation. I think it's probably more depression than cynicism, and more introspection with my own thoughts than anything else. Perhaps it's mostly remembering how much you and Pa absolutely

relished synagogue services at the end of a hard week's work.

"I am worried about 'infecting' the children with my religious sobriety and lack of fundamentalist fervor. On the contrary, I want them to be as enchanted with our religion as they can. There is time enough for disenchantment. I want them to have a very positive feeling for religion to pass on to their own children and to face tragedy with, in future years. But I would also want them to know and learn to live with the fact that religion cannot provide all the answers to all the questions, and that there are many things in life which will always remain inexplicable.

"I don't believe that the Holocaust was part of a Divine plan leading to the creation of the State of Israel. And I don't believe your murder has any hidden meaning. You were in the wrong place, at the wrong time, and you had a battle-zone mentality, which was fatal. Everything went wrong that night. There's no reason and no meaning for what happened. If I could avenge your death, I would. Even the police can't seem to do that, and if G-d ever does, we'll probably never know it.

"I will miss your letters, Yitz, and sharing my life with you. Having you as my brother was a rare gift, and the older I got, the more I appreciated you. Perhaps sharing these letters with other people will allow them to appreciate you too, and understand my pride. So many good people like you pass away, leaving only a tombstone for later generations to guess who they were, and who loved them. I really couldn't let you go without filling in just a little portion of the middle of the stone. Your loving brother, Eliezer"

Yitz left behind his wife, Miriam, and four children -- Debby, Daniel, David and Ruth. Over time, everyone in the family immigrated to Israel, with Eliezer accompanying them and serving as a bridge to help connect them to their new land. Debby, the eldest

daughter, was already married to Arnie and had a son at the time her father was murdered. She first came to Israel in 1970 as part of Bnei Akiva *hachshara* (year in kibbutz) and was hosted on Shabbatot (Sabbaths) at the Jaffe home in Jerusalem.

She returned to her parents' home in Cleveland when the year was up, but later she made aliya and studied social work at the Hebrew University. She married Arnie in the third year of her studies. The couple returned to the United States for Arnie to finish his studies there, but they decided to return to Israel before their eldest son went into the first grade.

And so it was. In 1983, Debbie and Arnie returned to Israel with two children. Daniel and David, the sons of Yitz and Miriam, came for a gap-year of study to the Yeshivat Kerem B'Yavneh, a *hesder* yeshiva (a yeshiva in which young men study and also go to the army for a shorter time-period than regular soldiers). The home of their Uncle Eliezer in Jerusalem was also, for them, the first stop in the country, and a warm home for them at all times. Daniel made aliya to Israel with his wife Barbara, and their daughter, in 1982.

David left MIT to move home and be supportive, continuing his college studies at Case Western Reserve, to be local, in Cleveland. In 1980 he made aliya to Israel with his wife Bracha. When the fourth daughter, Ruth, also started talking about her plan to move to Israel after graduating from high school, Miriam Jaffe decided it was time for her, too, to make aliya.

In 1983, Miriam fulfilled her late husband's dream, immigrated to Israel and settled in the apartment next to the home of Eliezer and Rivka, which was purchased before Yitz's murder.

A social worker by profession, Miriam began working at the Feuerstein Institute in Jerusalem and later also worked as a student counselor at the Hebrew University. Yitz was later commemorated

in the central synagogue of the Alon Shvut community in Gush Etzion, which was one of the first synagogues built in Judea and Samaria. Today his daughter Ruth Lieberman and her family live in the community, as well as his niece Dena Hirschfield – Alvin's daughter -- and her family.

Yitz's family were not the only ones who moved to Israel. Eliezer's other nephews, the children of his two brothers and sister, who remained in the United States, immigrated to Israel over the years. Allan, Alice's son, and his first wife, Amalia, immigrated to Israel in 1977. Elliot and Dena, Alvin's children, also made aliya with their families. Eliezer took great joy in every niece and nephew who made aliya, and was sure to accompany them in the process to help make the integration process as easy as possible.

When Allan, the first nephew, came on aliya in 1977, Eliezer wrote to his brother: "I am really very happy to see my nephew here after eighteen years of me being a bridgehead for our family. I've given up on Jack and Alvin but if I live long enough, chances are I will get to see a good representation of their children and who knows? It is possible that the children will lead their parents to the Promised Land."

During his last year of life, Eliezer was privileged to recite one of the seven blessings (*sheva brachot*) under the huppa of his brother's granddaughter, Leora, who was the first one of Jack's descendants to immigrate to Israel. After her an additional grandson of Jack's made aliya – Gabriel. At her wedding, Leora said that she was happy to be blessed by her "Israeli grandfather." About two years after Eliezer passed away, Leora and her husband, Noam, gave birth to their first child, a son.

The name they gave to their son, on a bright summer morning, was Moshe Eliezer.

## Chapter Eight

## Giving an Equal Opportunity

In 1977 Eliezer was appointed chairman of the admissions committee of the School of Social Work. The appointment occurred in the wake of the criticism that he expressed regarding the admissions procedures. Eliezer had been troubled for some time regarding the composition of the student body. It bothered him that close to 90% of the students were of Ashkenazi descent, and in contrast, more than 80% of the citizens for whom they were caring were of Sephardic descent.

In a critical article that he published on this topic, he claimed that the problem lay in the fact that the only criteria for admission to the School of Social Work were the results of matriculation and psychometric tests. Since a thousand applicants were competing for 120 places, the competition was stiff, and the applicants with the highest scores in these tests were the ones who were accepted. The solution he suggested was to also accept students with lower test scores, but who had high motivation to learn, in order to give them also an opportunity to study the profession.

Some of Eliezer's colleagues did not like the article. They claimed it suggested that the school discriminated against Sephardic applicants. But Eliezer was not claiming that there was intentional

discrimination, only that the rules of acceptance, that focused solely on prior academic achievements, caused many of the Sephardic applicants, who had studied in weaker schools, to not be competitive with a majority of the Ashkenazi applicants who studied in stronger schools, and who therefore had achieved higher scores.

## Chapter Nine

## The Rights of the Neighborhoods

One of the studies that occupied Eliezer in the 1970s and 1980s was the evacuation of the old Yemin Moshe neighborhood in Jerusalem. Yemin Moshe was established in 1891 as part of the process of the Jews leaving the walls of the Old City. It was established next to the Mishkenot Sha'ananim neighborhood and was named after the Jewish philanthropist Moshe (Moses) Montefiore, the owner of the land. The neighborhood was abandoned during the War of Independence, after which it was resettled by new immigrants from Turkey and Kurdistan.

For 19 years, the neighborhood was close to the municipal border line that crisscrossed the city and separated between the Israeli and Jordanian sides. Following the unification of two parts of Jerusalem during the Six Day War, Yemin Moshe changed from being a neighborhood on the periphery, to becoming a neighborhood in the center of reunited Jerusalem. This change in status led the government to decide to change the character of the neighborhood, and turn it into a quarter of artists, academics and writers. To this end, the East Jerusalem Development Company, that was established to develop the neighborhoods between the Old City and the new city, decided to initiate the eviction of Yemin Moshe residents, in order to

absorb a new population that would include artists and professionals and residents from abroad.

In 1968, Finance Minister Pinchas Sapir decided to expropriate the neighborhood's land.

The veteran residents of the neighborhood were asked to leave their homes for other neighborhoods in Jerusalem in exchange for financial compensation that would help them purchase alternative apartments. But they were not happy about being evicted from their homes and resisted the move. The issue reached a discussion in the Knesset and with the State Comptroller, who examined the affair and found many defects in the process of the eviction and the repopulating of the neighborhood.

In the wake of a report filed by a veteran social worker in southern Jerusalem about a significant increase in the number of requests to her office from among the families evicted from the Yemin Moshe neighborhood, Eliezer suggested to a group of social work students, who were about to graduate, that they investigate and write a study on the topic.

In the study, that was conducted during 1972, two parallel groups were examined. One was a group of families of veteran tenants who had not yet been evicted from the neighborhood, and a second group was a group of families who had been evicted from it. Eliezer's students discovered that, from the social perspective, only a few of the evicted were satisfied with their new place of residence. Many evacuees expressed bitterness and feelings of frustration. They claimed to have received "zero" compensation for their homes and expressed dissatisfaction with their replacement apartments. An examination of the economic situation of the evacuees found that close to half of the evicted, who did not have debts while living in the neighborhood, plunged into high debt after being evicted from it.

The researchers also compared the economic situation of the residents who were evicted from the neighborhood to the residents who remained in it and found that eighty percent of the evacuees had significantly higher debts than those who remained. Although 60% of those remaining in the neighborhood also had debts, the sums were quite low. It also turned out that half of the evicted moved to poor neighborhoods in Jerusalem.

In addition to the economic findings and the evacuees' stance on the matter, Eliezer's researchers found that the [state] institutions did not create socio-cultural and economic conditions for the rehabilitation of the evicted and no uniform criteria were set for compensation. The main conclusion of the researchers was that the eviction of the residents of Yemin Moshe was not done in order to rehabilitate the residents, who belonged to a lower socio-economic stratum, but to evacuate the area for the benefit of the affluent who subsequently settled in the neighborhood.

The students' report was publicized at the end of December, 1972, and engendered a public outcry. A few days later, Eliezer received a letter from lawyers representing the East Jerusalem Development Company, threatening to take legal action and demanding that they receive the full study. Eliezer responded with his own letter in which he recommended that the Development Company review the study and not rely on newspaper articles. Even after reading the study, the Company's people claimed that they had acted in the framework of the legal tools that were made available to them and, in addition to that, they doubted the credibility of the study's conclusions.

As a result of the study, another front of attack was opened with Mayor Teddy Kollek. About two months after the study was published, Kollek accused the university's School of Social Work of "giving its name to unscientific work feeding from dubious sources."

Kollek claimed that the research work was cheap sensational material and the personal revenge of Eliezer against the Jerusalem municipality following his dismissal from the Welfare Department, nine months earlier.

But Kollek's claim did not match the time frames. The students' study about the evicted from Yemin Moshe, that was done under the guidance of Eliezer, began a long time before Eliezer left the municipality. Eliezer argued that there was no connection between the study and his allegedly personal wish to take revenge for his firing. He claimed that as a researcher and social worker dealing with welfare issues, his motives are purely scientific and societal and the use of the revenge claim is an attempt to try to make the research appear as if it was conducted with a personal agenda.

Mayor Kollek presented a report that had been prepared by an economist who was hired privately by the East Jerusalem Development Company, in which it was claimed that the study was biased, prejudiced and devoid of any professional plan to improve the situation. Eliezer responded to the economist's report by claiming that it was based on a slanted agenda. He responded to all the economist's claims against the study and even suggested to him and to the municipality that other researchers, acceptable to Mayor Kollek, conduct additional research on the neighborhood.

If the facts presented in our study were controversial, Eliezer argued, the East Jerusalem Development Corporation and municipality would have had to conduct an independent study about the evacuees from the neighborhood and the processes they went through, in order to resolve the disagreements. Eliezer also claimed, relying on the State Comptroller's report, that the evicting parties did not implement the decisions of the Ministerial Committee on Jerusalem Affairs in everything regarding the alternate housing offered to the evacuees.

In early March, 1973, an article about the study was published in the Jerusalem Post. Mayor Kollek was quoted as saying that the publication of the study led by Eliezer caused a lot of damage and harmed further restoration plans in the city. In response to an article published by Eliezer in the newspaper, he referred to the accusations made against him and against the researchers, and claimed that the damage that Kollek was talking about was merely financial damage, as the neighborhood residents who had not yet been evicted, raised their demands from the Development Company and the municipality, in the wake of the study.

The study on Yemin Moshe succeeded in provoking a public debate about the expropriation of land in the neighborhood. Many argued that the expropriation was not done for public needs but mainly for the needs of those with considerable means from abroad.

"What is so sacred about this great project?" Eliezer wondered in an interview with Yedioth Ahronoth. "It started as a nice thing – an artists' quarter, and became a neighborhood of the wealthy who were recruited to rehabilitate the area. Rehabilitation of the neighborhood does not justify expelling the poor and bringing in the rich. Why was it not possible to rehabilitate the neighborhood and leave the old tenants?" Eliezer also rejected the claim that if the veteran tenants had stayed, it would have remained a poor neighborhood. "I am of the opinion that if people live in a respectable place, they learn to respect it," he said. "I know it's first and foremost a question of money, but if the government is interested in rehabilitating people, then rehabilitate them in their place of residence, not a little bit at a time but in one big operation. It could have been an interesting experience."

Journalist Gideon Alon summed up the debate over the study in Haaretz in the following words: "The general impression of objective

people involved in the subject, with whom I spoke, is that Dr. Jaffe's research is more thorough and reasoned than the survey conducted by a private economist whose aim was to discredit the arguments that emerged from the study done by [the students of] the School of Social Work."

The reverberations of the research led by Eliezer subsided a bit over time, but it also affected public discourse in later years. Residents of the Nachlaot neighborhood in Jerusalem and the Yad Eliyahu neighborhood in Tel Aviv, who were earmarked for rehabilitation and eviction, claimed that they would not be like the residents of Yemin Moshe but would stand up for their rights, and would demand to return to the neighborhood after its rehabilitation.

Eliezer also began to receive many personal inquiries from families from different parts of the country who were asked to vacate their homes for various reasons. The families sought help, support and advice from him on how to stand up for their rights so as not to become victims of [the perceived needs of] society. In the legal area, the study led to the issuance of an important directive according to which the expropriation of land for public purposes will not include the construction of single-family buildings. Also, if the land is suitable for the construction of single-family buildings, it will be handed over first to the landowners who have been evacuated.

In 1980, seven years after the first study was done on Yemin Moshe, Eliezer returned to research the story of the neighborhood. In the study he directed, students surveyed the situation in the neighborhood after its rehabilitation and resettling in order to determine if the goal for which it was evacuated was realized. Most of the residents in the neighborhood already lived there about five years. In a questionnaire that was distributed to them, the factors that were examined were the economic situation of the residents,

the demographics of the population and the image that the neighborhood had in the eyes of its residents.

The researchers succeeded in interviewing less than half of the families because most of them weren't home. Eliezer estimated that the high percentage of absenteeism from the neighborhood was a result of the fact that the research took place during the winter and that was the time that many of the neighborhood's residents, for whom their houses were summer homes, were not in Israel.

The results of the study showed that the percentage of people originally from the West and from within Israel, who lived in Yemin Moshe, was twice as large as their percentage among the population in Israel, while the percentage of the population from Asia and Africa in the neighborhood was three times smaller than their population in Israel.

It turned out that Yemin Moshe had become a mostly Ashkenazi neighborhood, with only 14% of the residents being of Sephardic descent. In addition, 35% of the residents in the neighborhood were citizens of European countries or America or had dual citizenship. The residents had a much higher level of education than the national average, the majority were academicians and about a fifth of the residents did not even [have to] work. In spite of the fact that the neighborhood was founded with the express aim that it will be an artists' quarter, only a fifth of the residents were artists. From an examination of the financial situation of the residents, it appeared that it had become a neighborhood with affluent residents.

A few of those who remained in the neighborhood after the eviction expressed sadness to the researchers about the change in the character of the area and its residents. They complained of cold neighborly relations and not enough pleasant interaction between the residents.

Eliezer drew a number of conclusions from his research on the Yemin Moshe neighborhood. The first was that the neighborhood was physically rehabilitated and became a tourist attraction, but the move was purely economic and it was highly doubtful that it morally justified the expropriation of land in the neighborhood and the eviction of residents for what was defined as "public purposes."

At the same time, Eliezer found that the initial research on the neighborhood and the public debate that ensued had a positive effect on the East Jerusalem Development Company's conduct toward the neighborhood's veteran residents. The residents felt a greater degree of openness and willingness to help and the social workers received fewer complaints. The researchers who visited the company's offices were positively impressed by the social responsibility and care that was given to the evicted families. Eliezer saw this as proof of the great importance of public involvement in issues such as urban planning and neighborhood rehabilitation.

Despite the negative reactions of the East Jerusalem Development Company and the Jerusalem municipality to his research, Eliezer argued that public projects are legitimate goals for research and that public discussions about the findings of the research are essential and inevitable. "Researchers should not be deterred from investigating politically, socially and economically sensitive issues and they should not be afraid of attempts to curb their research through silencing," Eliezer wrote. "While there may be differences in how the findings are interpreted, it is important to publish the facts revealed in order to receive responses from the public and from colleagues in the profession .... Without publication and controversy there will be no discussion and no progress in studying the subject."

An additional conclusion reached by Eliezer was the necessity of providing legal advice to the residents who are about to be evicted in

order to ensure that they will take the maximum advantage possible of the legal system to safeguard their rights. He was even convinced that if legal advice is not easily obtainable by them, it is a service that should be built into the law even at the expense of a government office.

Eliezer's last conclusion, and perhaps the most important, was that the renewal of a neighborhood should not necessitate the eviction of the original residents and the exchanging of them with other residents. He was convinced that a neighborhood should have been established in Yemin Moshe that would be ethnically and socio-economically diverse, that would include both veteran and new residents, and that would enable everyone to enjoy their renovated homes. This stance of his came from the belief that urban renewal should not only renew the houses but also the lives of their dwellers, that it should be not only physical rehabilitation but also social rehabilitation.

In 1985, Eliezer published the book "Yemin Moshe - The Story of a Jerusalem Neighborhood." In the book, he described the changes that took place in the neighborhood from its establishment until after its restoration, after the Six Day War, and the replacement of its population with affluent residents. Eliezer included photos taken by his daughter Yael (and did not forget to give her credit). Eliezer chose to conclude the book with the following sentences: "It seems that today we must thank Moshe Montefiore and Judah Touro, who purchased this plot of land, about 130 years ago, with significant financial input and with the purest aspirations to alleviate the plight of their brothers who were languishing in substandard conditions in the Old City. It is doubtful that they would have *nahat* (pleasure) from the sight they would see here today!"

Eliezer's studies on the Yemin Moshe neighborhood, that began

in the early 1970s, became especially relevant with the birth of the national project of Neighborhood Restoration at the end of the same decade. In 1977 a political upheaval took place in Israel. The Likud party replaced Labor in power and Menachem Begin was appointed Prime Minister. One of the first welfare programs of Begin was that of Neighborhood Restoration. In the framework of that program, he asked the government to restore 160 neighborhoods in Israel over the next five years

Eliezer was pleased with the plan and was convinced that it was mandatory but he also had criticism about its initial design. He published an article in the newspaper in which he raised some of his qualms. First of all, he argued that the plan to restore 160 neighborhoods within five years was not feasible. "Even if the government is able to raise the money within that time period, we don't have any proven examples of the time demanded to restore a poor neighborhood, including coordinating between the local, regional and national authorities who would be involved in the project, and the combining of social services together with the housing."

Secondly, he said, the restoration should take place together with the cooperation of the residents. "Neighborhoods, like people, have souls. Is there anyone among the planners who took the trouble to get to know the 'souls' of the 160 neighborhoods earmarked for restoration?...Who spoke with the neighborhood committees or with their service suppliers?"

Eliezer suggested dedicating at least one year to deal with four or five neighborhoods and to develop them as an example of physical and social restoration, including the cooperation of all those involved. "Even if only three years will remain till the next elections, one must assume that the public will appreciate the good beginning in the area of housing. Far-ranging promises that cannot be fulfilled

will harm those who made those promises, no matter the reasons or who is to blame."

In the end, to Eliezer's joy, the neighborhood restoration project included not only physical restoration but also economic social restoration. In addition, the project refrained from evicting residents from their homes and included them in decision making, in contrast to what was done during the restoration of Yemin Moshe. Eliezer saw a clear connection between the social and ethnic struggle that was manifested in the political upheaval and between the way in which the neighborhood restoration project was conducted. He believed that the political rise of the Sephardic population in Israel brought with it a change in the perception of urban renewal and neighborhood restoration and that what happened with Yemin Moshe would not repeat itself.

Eliezer's special contribution to the neighborhood restoration project, according to David Bedein, his devoted student, was the idea of twinning Jewish and philanthropic communities in America with neighborhoods and cities in Israel that were included in the project.

In practice, Eliezer's idea of matchmaking suggested that Jewish communities abroad take it upon themselves to adopt the restoration of a particular neighborhood in Israel. The local authority of the adopted neighborhood would present the adopting community with a request for the funding of the restoration project. The leadership of the adopting community would examine the plan, approve it, and accompany its implementation.

The idea of matchmaking-adoption met a number of needs and served several purposes. Eliezer believed that Diaspora Jews wanted to feel more involved in social action in Israel. He believed that such a partnership would be created as a result of donors from abroad

becoming personally acquainted with neighborhood leaders, by tours of Diaspora Jews in the neighborhoods, by their involvement in decisions and by their direct contribution of funds to locations destined for restoration, without the help of intermediaries.

As an example of the success of this model, Eliezer brought the factory of the Ablat family from New York, who adopted the Galilee town of Hatzor HaGlilit, and who badgered all senior officials in Israel with their demands for the provision of essential services to Hatzor.

Indeed, the matchmaking program proposed by Eliezer was adopted by the government and proved successful. The connection between the communities abroad and neighborhood leaders created a direct, fruitful and efficient connection between the donors and the neighborhood leaders. This matchmaking also established the rehabilitation project financially. It did not have to rely solely on state budgets, thus securing its future.

In June 1981, four years after the 1977 political upheaval, elections were held again, in which the Likud also won. Menachem Begin continued in his position as prime minister and his government continued the neighborhood rehabilitation project. At the end of this government's term, Eliezer was interviewed by the journal "The Academic" and commented on the results of the project. "In my opinion, this is one of the relatively successful stories in the social sphere. 50% of the rehabilitation budget comes from abroad and 50% comes from our taxes or from existing services that have been 'stolen' from other neighborhoods and put into neighborhood rehabilitation, to cover our 50%. We ended up with close to 40,000 families living in poor neighborhoods who we had forgotten for a long time due to the various waves of immigration and other problems. "

Eliezer also related to the ethnic aspect of the project and

mentioned that the neighborhoods that were restored in the framework of this project were those in which lived mostly people of Sephardic descent who lived in difficult conditions. He claimed that the rehabilitation of the neighborhoods helped Likud receive the votes of many Sephardic people in the elections to the Knesset. And still, Eliezer wanted to remind everyone that the success of the neighborhood restoration project would be assessed at the end. He claimed that the real test would be in the local leadership that emerged from the neighborhoods, in the reaction of the donors from abroad who gave hundreds of millions of dollars to the program, and in the ability of the cities to continue the rehabilitation program.

In the same interview, Eliezer also spoke about the necessity for citizens, and especially academics, to be socially involved. "Every citizen must contribute to society and it is not enough that he receives a salary as an employee somewhere, but he must find the place to contribute as a volunteer -- with his knowledge, with his energy, with his ideas for problems that trouble Israeli society. Those who studied the social sciences and humanities should be especially troubled, as they are expected to understand the significance of social issues and flashpoints in society.

"It is a moral imperative for the citizen, and especially for the university graduate, to give to others and to give to Israeli society. In my opinion, this imperative is moral and it is also in his soul. If everyone waits for the politicians to save the country, we will wait a long time. I think that the citizen is obligated to become involved in social projects, and to help move them forward, as a volunteer, to the greatest extent possible.

"The nature of the country depends to a great extent on us. This is not just a matter of choosing for whom to vote at the ballot box, and it is not enough to read in the news about how others are running the

country, but it is an issue of personal work and individual involvement in issues. In every place that we work, each of us must do his share. It would be a shame here in Israel, with all that goes on, to not take part in some way in these matters. This could unfortunately be a missed opportunity."

## Chapter Ten

## For the Good of the Child

In 1983, Eliezer published the book "Israelis in Institutions: Studies in Child Placement, Practice and Policy," in which he compiled all his research on Israeli children living in institutional boarding schools[9]. For historical, economic and cultural reasons, the way of helping children in need of guardianship that developed in Israel in the first decades of the state was placing them in these institutions.

The percentage of children in Israel referred to institutional placement was the highest in any country in the world. There were many benefits in taking children from distressed families and placing them in boarding schools but there was also a price to be paid for it. Some of the institutions were large and far away from the children's homes and this created a disconnect between the children and their families. When Eliezer began his research in the field shortly after he made aliya, he was impressed by the dedication of social workers who cared for these children, but he was less impressed by the lack of information about services provided to children in institutions, and by the excessive Influence of outsiders on policy and planning

---

9     These are not to be confused with regular educational boarding schools, that also existed at the time (and still exist).

in this area. In many cases, the institutions were used as a tool for instilling a particular ideology and educational philosophy into the children, and sometimes this goal came at the expense of the child's needs and well-being.

Eliezer saw his book not only as a presentation of research but also as providing a voice for the children in the institutions. In the introduction to the book, he wrote that the more he researched the issue of placement in institutions, the more it became clear to him that these children were not able to talk about their condition.

"None of these children - from the toddlers in the nurseries to the intelligent teenagers in the institutions - are given the opportunity to express their views on the social policies that concern them," he wrote. "Moreover, children have almost no contact with people outside the placement system who can present the facts to outsiders." In his studies, which were groundbreaking in this field, Eliezer examined the history of institutional care, the bodies that decide on placement in the institution, and the effects that staying in the institution had on the young people and their relationship with their families. Eliezer presented the treatment in institutions both from the perspective of the treating staff and from the perspective of the children in their care. He also examined the services provided in Israel in order to determine how placement in an institution could be reduced or prevented.

One of the important findings that emerged from Eliezer's research was regarding the feelings of the children in the institutional boarding schools. According to Eliezer's research, the children were not sufficiently aware of the reasons for their placement in the institution, their future was vague, and the connection with their natural family was weak.

These feelings caused the children to not have enough confidence

in themselves and in their chances of future success. Eliezer also found that a large proportion of staff in the institutional boarding schools were unable to relate to children personally due to a shortage of staff and high turnover. The aim of the institutions was mainly educational but the emotional needs of the children were neglected.

"Conceptually, the principals perceived the role of these boarding schools as a way to provide protection, and as a way to provide the children with an education and to teach them social and national values that would help them to become educated and responsible citizens. All the roles involved in personal counseling, family ties and long-term goals were perceived as the area of operation of the social workers employed by the Ministry of Labor and Social Welfare."

At the end of his research, Eliezer wrote that in his opinion it was time to seriously examine alternatives to mass institutional care that was established as the main solution for children in need of care and in need of protection.

The main alternative he proposed was to strengthen the children's natural family systems and community services, rather than the mass sending of children to institutions, without enough oversight. "The State of Israel must now move resolutely and quickly towards strengthening community services for families in need and do everything in its power to help parents and families deal with their problems. This means investing in families, and not just in individual children, but more manpower for social and educational services, and better housing for many families."

This call by Eliezer, to reduce the removal of children from their homes, has over the years become a common perception among the welfare authorities in Israel. In many ways, in this area also, he was ahead of his time.

Along with Eliezer's call for expanding social services and

reducing placement in institutions, he also examined the quality of care that children and adolescents receive in institutions, and identified serious problems of unnecessary placements, staying beyond the necessary time, isolating children from their families and from social workers, and providing inappropriate treatment. In order to solve these problems, he called for the establishment of a public inter-ministerial committee that would supervise the institutions, critique the quality of care and work to raise the level of personnel working in the institutions.

In a review published of the book "Israelis in Institutions" in the magazine of the Social Workers' Union, Dr. Anita Weiner from the School of Social Work at the University of Haifa wrote that reading the book is a must for the thousands of workers in the field. "The book has a rare combination of research objectivity and moral involvement," Weiner wrote.

In another review, published in the journal "Trends," Dr. Tovah Lichtenstein wrote that it is a book of great importance in the field of child welfare in Israel. "There are few books that relate directly to what is happening in the field, and that report on the Israeli reality. Professor Jaffe's effort to investigate what is happening in the field and to provoke discussion on the subject," Lichtenstein wrote, "is a contribution to social work in the country in general and to the welfare of the child in particular."

In parallel with the book "Israelis in Institutions," Eliezer also published the book "Child Welfare in Israel" in English that year. The book was intended for those interested in and engaged in social services for children and families in need in Israel. He reviewed the history of foster care, adoption, boarding school arrangements, day care, income support and home care and summarized the research that had been done in each area. In this book, too, Eliezer reiterated

his idea that every action and every service done for the welfare of the child must relate to the good of the whole family, and not only to the good of the child, for only in this way can the good of the child truly be achieved.

In 1983, Eliezer published the book "Letters to Yitz." Unlike his books which were the results of research, it was a very personal book, in which Eliezer published some of the long-standing correspondence he had with his brother Yitz who had been murdered five years earlier. The moving correspondence between Eliezer and his brother beautifully reflected the story of their lives. The letters described the history and expansion of the family, the happy and tragic events that befell the brothers and the way they responded to each of the events. Eliezer included in his letters his insights into Israeli society, and experiences from his research and practical work and from his social enterprises. Many of the letters related also to national events that had taken place during the first three decades of the establishment of the State of Israel.

Eliezer and his brothers' different places of residence, in Israel and the United States, gave the events diverse and interesting angles. Most of all, the book "Letters to Yitz" revealed the deep love and appreciation that existed between the two brothers. The book "Letters to Yitz," published in Hebrew and English, has been read over the years by thousands of people, Jews and non-Jews, around the world. Some Jewish schools have even used it to study Jewish literature. Eliezer never imagined that so many people would feel a deep identification with his family story. For him, every reader of the book was like a memorial candle and raised a banner in memory of and in honor of his older brother.

The publication of the book "Letters to Yitz" was also a therapeutic process for Eliezer, in which he dealt with the loss of his

brother. Eliezer later said this to Dr. Bilha Bachrach, a social worker and lecturer at the School of Social Work at the Hebrew University. Bachrach had lost her son Ohad, a soldier, in a terror attack that took place in Wadi Kelt in 1995. After the loss of her son, she studied film at the Maaleh Film School and directed a film about his murder, called, "By Way of the Wadi." One evening she screened the film before the group of retired social workers, and Eliezer sat in the first row.

At the conclusion of the screening, Eliezer went to Bachrach and said to her, "There was indeed a therapeutic process here."

"I opposed that description," says Bachrach. "And I told Eliezer and the other people who claimed this, that I was the director of the film, that I was in charge of the shooting angles, I produced the film, but it was not treatment.

"Eliezer told me about the book 'Letters to Yitz' that he wrote in the wake of his brother's murder and he told me that the writing of the book was also therapy for him." Bachrach decided to listen to the words of Eliezer and others, and began to study the topic. She wrote her doctorate on the subject of memorial films that were created by bereaved parents in memory of their children. In her work she analyzed the way in which people choose to tell their story, and how the way they choose responds to different ways of dealing with bereavement.

In the year the book "Letters to Yitz" was published, Eliezer turned fifty and he was already a renowned researcher and a well-known social activist. Two years earlier, in 1981, he had been promoted from senior lecturer to associate professor. Rivka continued her work at the Jerusalem branch of MATAV and also continued to advance her education. She took a course in geriatrics at the School of Medicine and took a course on guiding students, in the framework

of continuing education at the Hebrew University. The children also grew up. Uri finished his high school studies at Yeshivat Bnei Akiva Or Etzion in Merkaz Shapira and enlisted in the Golani Brigade. After his release from the army, he followed in his parents' footsteps and chose to study social work.

He chose not to do so at the Hebrew University but at Bar Ilan University, in order to pave an independent professional path for himself. But even among the faculty at Bar Ilan, many of the lecturers knew and admired Eliezer. Some were even familiar to Uri from meetings they had with his father in his home.

In the first year of his studies, Uri met Keren Yarkoni, who was also studying social work at Bar Ilan University. To this day, Keren remembers her excitement from the initial meeting with Eliezer, "The Professor of Social Work." From her first visit to Uri's home, she remembers Eliezer sitting and writing at his desk in the study, surrounded by piles of pamphlets and books. On October 5, 1984, the 9th of Tishri, 5745, at the beginning of the second year of their studies, Uri and Keren were married and established a home. Not long after, their eldest son Roi was born to them, making Eliezer and Rivka grandparents.

Yael, the second daughter of Eliezer and Rivka, chose to study medicine after her military service and Eliezer and Rivka were very happy with her choice. When Naomi and Ruti finished their military service, they chose to study psychology. Thus, unsurprisingly, the four children of Eliezer and Rivka chose to study and engage in social professions, which provide assistance to people. The parents did not direct them to these professions, but the love for people and the desire to help, solve problems, and contribute to society was embedded deep in the walls of the Jaffe family. The parents instilled in their children the confidence that the world is good and that human

beings are good. They instilled in them an optimism that helped them naturally choose professions that deal with people, in order to add good to the world.

In September, 1986, members of the Zahavi movement, together with the Jaffe family, held an evening honoring Eliezer in the style of the TV show "This is Your Life" which dealt with the lives of various personalities known for the part they played in the country's history and culture.

The event took place on the occasion of Eliezer going on sabbatical and as a gesture of gratitude for his work to advance the Zahavi organization. As in the TV show, the evening was organized without Eliezer's knowledge and those invited to it were asked to keep it a secret. At the beginning of the evening, the moderator said: "Every person's aliya to Israel is an adventure and only the sabras have a hard time understanding that. Usually, one who has succeeded in moving from one world to another reaches his destiny rich in experience but having lost his illusions along the way.

"One of a kind is our friend Eli, known as Professor Eliezer Jaffe, who left the United States in his youth, studied and found his life's partner in Jerusalem, started a family and mentored many students in social work, and still abounds in innocent faith, faith in God and man."

The evening's organizers prepared a number of surprises for Eliezer. They invited his aunt and cousins to the event and also arranged a phone call between him and his brothers in the US. During the moving evening, Eliezer was praised by both his colleagues from the academic world and by his friends for his social activities at Zahavi and other organizations.

In 1987, Eliezer and Uri went on a special mission to Russia, "beyond the Iron Curtain." The government in Russia in those days was still

a communist regime of the Soviet Union, a regime that prevented Jewish activity and aliya to Israel. The Jewish Agency was looking for Israelis with American passports who could pass reading materials with Jewish and Zionist content to Jewish activists -- students and scientists who had been refused permission to immigrate to Israel. Jewish Agency personnel approached Eliezer to join the mission and he responded in the affirmative and asked Uri to join him.

From Israel, Eliezer and Uri flew to London, where they met with a Foreign Ministry official, who took their Israeli passports and any other Israeli identity cards from them, and equipped them with the reading materials they were asked to transfer. From London, Eliezer and Uri flew to Moscow with their American passports. The materials they were asked to transfer were hidden between the double walls of their suitcases. When they arrived in Moscow, they were taken, like any tourist at the time, straight from the airport to the hotel near Red Square.

In the briefing given to them before their departure, they were warned not to speak a word of Hebrew throughout their stay in the Soviet Union. Even in the hotel room they made sure to speak English for fear of eavesdropping. When they wanted to speak Hebrew, they did so by writing notes that were then flushed down the toilet. For three weeks, Eliezer and Uri met with Zionist activists in the cities of Moscow, Kiev and Leningrad and gave them the materials they had received from the Foreign Ministry officials. During one of the meetings, a warning was suddenly sounded about the arrival of the KGB, and Eliezer and Uri were required to disappear from the scene quickly.

Eliezer and Uri returned to Israel laden with exciting experiences and satisfied with the fulfillment of the Zionist mission imposed on them. Later, after the fall of the Iron Curtain in the Soviet Union,

they were excited to meet, in Israel, some of those who had been refused permission to emigrate, with whom they had met during their mission.

In the early 1990s, the Jaffe family grew. In August, 1991, Naomi married Ohad Eini. About a month later, Yael married Moshe Zimmerman. Four years later, Ruti married Udi Palmor. The children left the nest but very quickly the number of grandchildren began to grow and Eliezer greatly enjoyed his new status. He would sing to his grandchildren, tickle them and buy them toys. When they grew up a little, he would challenge them with riddles and watch cartoons with them, and it wasn't clear who enjoyed it more.

In the 1990s, Eliezer was one of the initiators of the legal regulating of adopting children from abroad. The issue of adoption as a whole occupied Eliezer for decades. When he was still in America in the 1950s, he became aware of problems regarding adoption in the framework of his training as a social worker in Cleveland, Ohio. Over the years he researched and published many articles on institutional care, foster care, and adoption and, as mentioned, in the early 1980s he also published a book on child placement policy in institutions.

The waiting time for the adoption of children in Israel in the early 1990s was an average of about seven years. The long wait of thousands of childless couples to adopt children in the country led many of them to look for the alternative of adopting children from other countries. The process of adopting children from abroad began in Israel in the mid-1970s to the early 1990s and thousands of children were adopted from various countries, mainly from South America and Eastern Europe. Eliezer wanted to examine the extent of the phenomenon based on his assumption that it would grow with the years. He predicted that as Israeli society will become more accepting of

single mothers, the number of adoption applicants would increase, the queue for adoption will become longer and the request for adoption of children from abroad would also increase accordingly. The Adoption Law enacted in 1981 did not apply to children adopted abroad and brought to Israel. Although the state recognized adoption performed abroad, the welfare services did not play a mediating role in the adoption process as they did in the adoption of children in Israel. Eliezer, who saw the adoption channel from abroad as a good solution to the high demand for adoption, was convinced that the adoption law should be amended so that it would also apply to the adoption of children from abroad.

To research the phenomenon, Eliezer published ads in newspapers and magazines and sought information from adoptive parent organizations, lawyers, and social workers about children adopted from abroad. Eventually he managed to reach fifty-six adoptive families. The study revealed that the children adopted abroad were usually adopted through the courts of the countries in which the adoptions took place and then they immigrated to Israel with their (new) parents, with a passport. The State of Israel did not have official adoption agreements with other countries. The study also revealed that most of the couples who adopted children abroad tried first to adopt a child in Israel but gave up in despair due to the long waiting period and the bureaucracy.

In the wake of the study, Eliezer went into action, together with a group of social workers, to copy the American model of adoption of children from foreign countries. In the American model, the process of adoption of the child could take place after his country of birth gave him permission to leave. At the time, Eliezer believed that reproducing this model in Israel would facilitate the adoption of foreign children and also reduce its costs.

After interviewing the parents who adopted children from abroad, Eliezer went on to study adoption in 14 different countries around the world during his sabbatical year. He also toured many orphanages in South America and Eastern Europe. When he entered orphanages, the children grabbed his legs and begged him to lift them up, hug them and stroke them. These difficult scenes reminded Eliezer of scenes that he saw in orphanages in Jerusalem thirty years earlier.

In addition to his visits to orphanages, Eliezer met with lawyers and social workers who accompanied adoption processes in those countries. He discovered that, unlike in Israel, in many countries there were private organizations that operated legally and made the international adoption process easy, cheap and simple. Israeli parents, on the other hand, had to make do without the help of reputable organizations and, as a result, often came into contact with dubious people.

As a social worker, Eliezer felt deeply ashamed that the State of Israel did not provide proper social services to couples adopting children abroad. The fact that the body that organized the adoption in Israel through the Ministry of Welfare was called "The Service for the Child" reflected, in his opinion, a distorted reality in which the Ministry of Welfare worried only about the welfare of the adopted children, and not about the distress of the couples who were childless.

After interviewing leading professionals in the field in each and every country, Eliezer asked each of the authorities in the field to write an article on the methods of adoption in his country. He published the results in a book entitled: "Intercountry Adoptions: Laws and Perspectives of 'Sending' Countries." The book was written in English because it was the language of the authors of the articles.

At a press conference held by Eliezer in February, 1993, he criticized the method of adoption in Israel and claimed that it turns adopting couples into victims, and forced parents to sometimes break the law because no one in the country dealt with the issue.

Eliezer said that some parents who apply for the adoption of children from foreign countries travel abroad without documents and without support and guidance, fall into the hands of crooks and thieves, and embroil themselves, the children, and the state in problems.

In some cases, children who were adopted in Israel [from foreign countries] were taken from the adoptive parents after a short time because the process was not done legally. One of these cases that received media attention was the story of the girl Bruna-Caroline Consuelus, a baby from Brazil who stayed with her adoptive parents for about a year before being returned to her biological mother; it later turned out that she had been abducted from her. Eliezer called for an amendment to the Adoption Law in Israel and to add elements relating to international adoption.

He argued that the amended law must provide parents who adopt children from abroad with the help they deserve, both through public services and through private organizations such as those operating in other countries. Eliezer was convinced that the reality in Israel at the time, in which the topic of adoption was managed entirely by a monopoly in the hands of "The Service for the Child" that operated under the Ministry of Welfare, was harmful to adoptive parents. He believed that the entry of private associations into the field of adoption would make the processes more efficient and would make it easier on the adoptive parents. In addition, he believed that the Service for the Child did not have the logistical capacity to manage international adoptions, which required operating a system of relations with many countries.

In May, 1993, an international convention on child protection and cooperation on international adoption was signed in The Hague, the Netherlands. The Hague Convention was based on international cooperation between the signatory countries. Its purpose was to ensure that international adoption would be carried out in accordance with the principle of the best interests of the child and would be conducted in a controlled and orderly manner, through the official authorities of the signatory countries. All this in order to prevent the phenomena of child abduction, smuggling and trafficking.

In November, 1993, the Israeli ambassador to The Hague signed the convention on behalf of the State of Israel, and in doing so, Israel undertook not to act in violation of the provisions of the convention. But beyond the signing, the State of Israel was required to adapt its adoption law to the new treaty and include in it a reference to international adoption. Eliezer recognized this as a great opportunity.

MKs Limor Livnat of the Likud and Anat Maor of the Meretz party, who heard and read Eliezer's remarks in the media, began working to amend the adoption law in Israel in the spirit of his views. Eliezer was very involved in drafting the new law and attended all the meetings of the Constitution and Law Committee that discussed its wording. At the end of the process, the amendment to the Adoption Law was enacted in 1996, and reference was made to international adoption. Attempts to make further amendments to the law delayed its final approval until January 1998.

In the early stages of the legislative process, the government opposed Eliezer's proposal that private non-profit organizations could write memoranda and actually implement the adoption process. As far as the government was concerned, the associations were only meant to provide information to parents. In the end, Eliezer's position, which won the support of Knesset members, overcame

objections and the law stipulated that the associations could carry out the adoption process themselves.

The law stipulates that international adoption will be carried out through an adoption association recognized by the Minister of Labor and Social Welfare and the Minister of Justice. The association will clarify the eligibility of the applicants who wish to adopt, contact the official authority of the country where the child to be adopted is located, and ensure that the process is implemented in accordance with all the certificates of approval and assessments accepted in that country. After all the approvals according to the law, the association will apply to the Minister of Interior to approve the entry of the adopted child into Israel.

Upon the child's entry to Israel, the adoption and conversion process of the child will be completed if his adoptive parents are Jews. In addition, the law stipulated that even after the parents return to Israel, contact with the adoption association will continue for at least another three years, a period during which the association must perform periodic inspections and follow-up, in order to report the child's condition to the adoption authorities in the foreign country and in Israel.

About two years after the final approval of the law, there were already 15 adoption organizations in Israel through which more than 600 children were brought to Israel. The adoption process itself had been shortened and simplified. Even after the amendment to the law, Eliezer found flaws in it. He argued that the maximum amount -- twenty thousand dollars -- set by law for each adoption procedure, should be increased and adapted to the conditions of each country, that the ban that prevented adoptive parents from disclosing to others that their child was adopted should be repealed, and that procedures should be established for dissolution of an adoption

association, if necessary. In addition, Eliezer claimed that after the associations proved their effectiveness in accompanying the adoption of children abroad, the adoption process in Israel should be allowed through associations and not just by the state.

## Chapter Eleven

## Giving Wisely

In the early 1980s, Eliezer began dealing with philanthropy in Israel. His acquaintance with this world had begun years earlier, as part of his work on welfare issues and with Zahavi.

At the end of the 1970s the number of NGOs or non-profit organizations (*amutot*)[10] grew exponentially, mostly due to Israel's transition from the economic policy of a welfare state to the policy of a market economy.

This economic policy included the reduction in government expenditure on social services and led to an increase of the "third sector"[11] and growth in the number of NGOs. In the early 1980s, there were 12,000 NGOs registered in Israel.

Eliezer's main motivation to engage in the field was the request of donors from Israel and abroad who wanted to consult with him. As someone who knew and dealt with social issues, they knew he could advise them regarding to which charities they should donate their money.

---

10  The terms "NGO," "non-profits," "associations," and "organizations," and "amutot" (the word in Hebrew) are used interchangeably.

11  The economic sector consisting of non-governmental organizations and other non-profit organizations.

"If I had a shekel for every philanthropist who wrote me, telephoned, or walked into my office at the Hebrew University's School of Social Work to ask my advice about 'where to contribute charity where it's really needed,' I could retire in style," Eliezer wrote in the introduction to his book "Giving Wisely."

On every one of Eliezer's visits to the United States, his relatives and friends showed him piles of letters sent to them by Israeli charities asking for donations. This occurred especially before the holidays -- Passover, Rosh Hashana, Chanuka and Shavuot. These letters included emotional requests for help, with return envelopes enclosed with P.O.B.s. When Eliezer saw this, he not only felt that these organizations were in need of support, but that the donors also needed help if they wanted to know how to work for Israeli society in the most direct and personal way.

First of all, he noted, the donors were missing information about the associations. Eliezer believed that they had the right to receive detailed information regarding all the organizations that asked them for assistance, and they also needed to know if the organization is officially recognized by Israeli authorities, what is the nature of its activities, who are the people who direct and manage it, and if donations are exempt from income tax.

Eliezer believed that detailed information about each organization could also lead to an increase in donations. He claimed that if the donors would have a deeper acquaintance with the associations, then rather than just throwing the letters away or sending a token amount, they may become excited about the various projects and contribute larger amounts.

"They may pull a specific emotional chord, answer a personal need of someone looking for a cause to support, and provide a vehicle to support that need," Eliezer wrote in the introduction to

"Giving Wisely." "Who has not wanted to memorialize the loss of parents and loved ones by undertaking a project in their name? Who has not wanted to leave some sign that we once existed here on this earth, and that we were not only out for ourselves while we were here? Who has been stirred by the miracle of Israel's rebirth and not sought to express some tangible measure of belonging and partnership in that magnificent enterprise? Perhaps one of those envelopes, piled high on the kitchen table, brings the opportunity to personalize one's relationship with Israel and its people, and to leave your footprint on our shores, however small."

This was how the book "Giving Wisely" came about -- the thirst for knowledge about these organizations led Eliezer to write it. He planned to include information about all the NGOs and non-profit associations in Israel. He saw the writing of this book as a service to both Jews and non-Jews, abroad and in Israel, who wanted to know more about these organizations, and he saw this as a way to make their philanthropic efforts more efficient.

The book was intended not just for the use of the donors but also for the organizations themselves. Eliezer's aim was to give a platform and an equal opportunity to all the non-profit associations in Israel. He wanted to describe their activities, to showcase their successes and their needs, and to familiarize them to potential donors abroad. The reality that he encountered in the philanthropic area was that only wealthy, sophisticated, and well-connected organizations, that knew how to manage public relations, succeeded in reaching large foreign audiences. In contrast, smaller organizations that didn't utilize the media and did not make strong connections with donors did not receive an equal and fair opportunity to get support and donations.

Some of the amutot didn't even know how to begin to raise money. Eliezer sensed that there was a need to connect between the amutot,

the volunteers, and the non-profit associations on the one hand, and the potential donors on the other. He believed that writing a guidebook for and about the amutot and the volunteer organizations would whet the appetite of both Jews and non-Jews, in Israel and abroad, and create in them a desire to get actively involved in the organizations in which they had an interest. He also thought it would create a direct and personal connection between the donors and Israelis who were seeking honest partnerships, expertise and funding.

There was another reason for writing the book about the non-profit associations. Eliezer's initiative also challenged the reality that had existed until then in the field of philanthropy. Most of the funds raised for Israel abroad were raised through the United Jewish Appeal[12] and Keren Hayesod. They transferred the funds to the Jewish Agency in Israel, and it transferred them to existing services and projects. Thus, the Jewish Agency had a monopoly on incoming philanthropy.

It was easy for donors abroad to deal with one "address" for their donations that was large and well-known, and not with hundreds of small and unknown associations. Eliezer, who was a warrior for justice, who wanted equal opportunities for all, believed that such a reality discriminated against associations and social organizations that do holy work but are not known to donors.

Another problem in this situation was the lack of personal and

---

12   When the UJA and CJF first merged, they operated under the name United Jewish Communities (UJC). In 2009, UJC changed its name to the Jewish Federations of North America (JFNA) to align more closely with the names of the majority of the Federations. JFNA is the legal successor of United Jewish Appeal, Inc. and The Council of Jewish Federations, Inc. (Source: https://jewishfederations.org/)

direct contact between the donors and the associations. Fundraising in a centralized manner through large and institutionalized bodies such as the UJA and Keren Hayesod, and the subsequent centralized distribution of funds by the Jewish Agency, created a disconnect between the donor and what was happening in the field. Eliezer believed that direct philanthropy encouraged more courageous partnerships, which may last longer than the bond formed when giving is through an intermediary.

Eliezer found additional disadvantages in the centralized transfer of funds through the Jewish Agency. The Jewish Agency transferred funds to a limited selection of social enterprises and also, in his opinion, involved quite a bit of politics in managing donors' money. Eliezer believed that there were worthy social bodies that did not receive support just because they were perceived as opposed to institutional thinking or were too independent of government oversight.

Eliezer also criticized the way in which Israel's welfare needs were presented by the UJA. He believed that they tended to present the needs in collective and stereotypical terms and generalizations about the elderly, the poor, and children, without explaining which people are included in these categories and what their needs are. Eliezer wanted the donors to receive as objective and detailed information as possible about the Israeli organizations asking for assistance. He wanted the donor public to cease to be a "captive audience" and the politicization of centralized Jewish philanthropy for Israel to cease.

Eliezer had the opportunity to take a closer look at how the funds were raised abroad while on a sabbatical in Cleveland. In November, 1974, Pinchas Sapir, who then served as chairman of the Jewish Agency, arrived in Cleveland to lecture to the local Jewish community and raise funds. Sapir's lecture was designed in a format of questions and answers. The interviewers were four members of the

community, including a representative of the Jewish Student Union in the city. The night before Sapir's lecture, a representative called Eliezer and told him bitterly that the organizers of the meeting had given him and his fellow students a series of humdrum questions to present to Sapir. The students refused to ask the questions offered to them and sought Eliezer's advice in formulating more serious questions.

Eliezer saw this story as a sign of contempt toward the Jewish community and a sad expression of an unhealthy relationship that had been nurtured for decades between representatives of the State of Israel and American Jewry.

In his many conversations with American Jews, he identified ignorance and shallow knowledge in everything regarding the social problems in Israel. He attributed this to the fact that the people of the UJA spoke first and foremost to their potential donors' emotion and not to their intellect, and dealt with generalities and not with specifics; they leaned on feelings and did not transmit accurate information or attempt to truly educate. Eliezer saw this as a poor and superficial way of raising funds and thought that it might empty all content from the connection between Israel and the Jews of the Diaspora.

Eliezer's feelings regarding this issue led him to be one of the initiators of the establishment of the New Israel Fund in the late 1970s. The foundation was established in California in 1979 by the couple Jonathan Cohen and Eleanor Friedman following feelings of alienation that they and their friends felt toward the United Jewish Appeal. The purpose of the fund was to include as many donors from abroad as possible to support grassroots organizations in Israel, without institutional mediation of the Israeli arm of the UJA. The first Israeli branch of the fund was established in 1980 and Eliezer

was appointed chairman of the fund's Israeli committee. Later, the fund changed the nature of its activities and moved from financial assistance only, to an integrated model of financing, counseling and guidance to promote social change. Eliezer was no longer involved in those stages.

As stated, Eliezer's decision to act for transparency in the field of non-profit organizations led him to initiate the Israeli guide for non-profit organizations in the fields of health, education and welfare. The first step he took was to send questionnaires to all the associations registered at the Ministry of Interior. In developing the questionnaire, Eliezer consulted with foreign philanthropists, with the Registrar of Associations, with the editors of the GuideStar [a guide for non-profits, today called "Candid" (https://candid.org/)] with the staff of the British Charity Commission, and with researchers from the third sector. The questionnaire included dozens of sections in identical versions in Hebrew and English and was accompanied by a letter of explanation and an envelope to return the questionnaire.

Eliezer's goal was to create for the donors a full and transparent profile of the associations including their history, organizational structure, goals, achievements, names of board members, financial status, scope of activities, people from abroad who recommend them, and information on the tax exemption issue. Eliezer did not ask the non-profit organizations to pay for their inclusion in the future guide. In preparing and publishing the guide, he was helped by foundations that funded the project and by a budget he received from the Hebrew University School of Social Work.

As expected, not everyone welcomed Eliezer's initiative. The transparency and direct giving that Eliezer sought to strengthen in the field of philanthropy threatened the intermediary bodies that

benefited from the fog and lack of knowledge that existed in the field. Various sources close to the United Jewish Appeal and the Jewish Agency warned Eliezer that the book he was about to publish would harm the UJA and the Jewish Agency's budget. He was told that donors abroad are not really interested in the truths put forth in a book like this and they don't need it. He was told that donors from abroad do not have time to learn in depth about the Israeli associations, that they are not interested in private and direct philanthropy, and that they trust their local Jewish leadership and their own professionals. People from the UJA were convinced that centralized giving was the best way to help Israel. They sent various emissaries to Eliezer to try to convince him to give up writing the book. One of them represented the UJA in New York. He met with Eliezer and claimed that publishing the book might interfere with the national fundraising effort in the U.S.

However, Eliezer, a determined social warrior, was not moved by the opposition of the UJA and the Jewish Agency nor by the emissaries sent to him. He thought that all the arguments were paternalistic and monopolistic, and they only convinced him even more of the necessity of the guide for non-profits. "The publication of 'Giving Wisely' is not intended to downplay the importance of the UJA-Federation Appeal (now, the 'United Jewish Communities') or its European counterpart, Keren Hayesod," Eliezer wrote. "There is no question in my mind that the centralized federation community campaigns are an important device to enable Jews around the world to tax themselves for local services and to identify in some degree with Israel and the Jewish people as a whole. The funds transferred to the Jewish Agency in Israel are utilized for important projects…

"Nevertheless, the lack of personal face-to-face involvement of most donors, the persistent appeal primarily to emotions rather than

to intellect, and the 'give-and-run' philanthropic style which is the hallmark of centralized fundraising, are simply not enough for a growing number of educated, committed, sophisticated, young and older philanthropists. These leaders want to work beyond their regular involvement with the mainstream Jewish fund-raising apparatus and want a personal stake in Israel, a partnership relationship. They want to see how their philanthropy is spent, they want much more control over it and more accountability for its use in Israel. They want to deal directly with real people in Israel, counterparts who they can trust, and whose energies they can cultivate for a better Israel. "

Due to their opposition to the guide, the members of the Jewish Agency refused to fill out the questionnaires sent to them by Eliezer, but in contrast, there were many associations that cooperated with Eliezer's initiative and invested a lot of time and thought in filling out the questionnaires. There were also organizations that wanted to maintain privacy and anonymity and those that did not want to mix "outside" funds with family funds that donated scholarships in memory of their loved ones.

There were organizations that did not want to disclose financial information that was requested in the questionnaire and there were also organizations that called Eliezer and asked to omit some of the information about the association. When Eliezer refused their request, they chose to not return the questionnaire to him at all.

In 1982, Eliezer published "Giving Wisely -- The Israel Guide to Non-Profit and Volunteer Organizations." The book was first published in English because its main target audience was donors abroad. The guide included 320 institutions and organizations that had filled out Eliezer's questionnaires.

Eliezer was aware that because the profile of the associations was

created using information that came from them, it also contained subjective and not just objective information. He knew he could not guarantee one hundred percent accuracy of the data and therefore suggested that donors, in addition to reading the association's profile in the book, ask to see official accountants' reports, visit the association's offices themselves, or through representatives, and find out all they can about the association.

In a critique of the book, Dov Genochovsky wrote in Kol Yerushalyim ("The "Voice of Jerusalem"): "This volume gives us the pictures as they are painted by the various organizations. It doesn't attempt to assess them, to prioritized them or to try to determine the truth of what is written by them – and it's good that way. Whoever knows how to read or whoever wants to read – let him read and assess and arrive at his own conclusions. It is possible that he will have questions before he opens his pocket and his wallet. Whoever does not investigate and does not demand answers or who does not donate anyway, is not in need of this book, but since we live in the midst of a mass attack, about what we have and what we don't have, we need this book. It has everything in it…everything that you will think of or not think of that is missing beneath our municipal sun.

"After all, one great rule in giving is already at our disposal: Are you listed there, in that book by Professor Jaffe? No? So why not? Do you have something to hide? Do you have something you do not want us to know or check? In short - those who are not there, do not deserve to be given a hand at all, unless you have some personal interest or personal trust in that particular supplicant. But do not settle for the fact that a particular association is listed in the book. You should also read what is written there below the listing itself. What appears in the self-portrait that the institution or organization paints about itself? Often, too often, you will find and be surprised

- and not necessarily for the better. Anyone who underestimates your intelligence to the extent that he does not even bother to camouflage his failures is certainly not worthy of being a partner in your income, even if he is listed there."

The book was a great success and found its way to the tables of many donors in Israel and abroad. In many states in the US it had a place of honor next to the blue tzedaka (charity) box of Keren Kayemeth LeIsrael, and became a popular guidebook for philanthropists, changing the map of donations to Israel. The exposure, for the first time, of scores of organizations that were thus far unknown, caused the donations to the UJA to drop and the donations to independent organizations, that dealt with specific issues, to rise.

Shortly after the nonprofit guide was published, an elderly Jew in a small town in Indiana called Eliezer and told him that he had a thousand dollars earmarked for donation. He was already thinking of transferring it to Hadassah Hospital, but decided to ask Eliezer first to which body Eliezer suggested that he donate. Eliezer suggested that he create an interest-free loan fund for families with many children to cover expenses such as textbooks, shopping for the holidays and home repairs. The man agreed, set up the fund and it grew over time, with the help of donations from other people, to a fund with $25,000.

Eliezer saw this story as an example of a small donation through which a bond of trust was established with the donor. He was convinced that if the money had been donated to Hadassah Hospital, it would not have made a significant difference, and that the establishment of this fund would give the donor greater satisfaction.

Another successful example was discovered by Eliezer -- a pair of stockbrokers from New York who contributed to the establishment of a zoo under the auspices of a psychiatric hospital in Safed. The

donation was born following a recommendation from one of the doctors who discovered that working with animals is of therapeutic value to patients. Eliezer gave this example as proof that a personal connection and trust, created between the donor and the body donated to, produces more effective donations.

Even the Jewish Agency, which feared Eliezer's guide, learned from the project and adapted to the new reality. Agency staff internalized the need for a more direct connection between donors and the field. In 1987, the Agency established a grant fund that provided millions of dollars to hundreds of projects that were implemented by hundreds of diverse non-profit associations. At the same time, prestigious funds began to be established whose lists of donors were based on the philanthropists' personal acquaintance with the organizations. Eliezer began to see how the book he published brought about change and achieved its goals.

## Chapter Twelve

## Partnership Philanthropy

In 1980, Eliezer published a booklet called "Pleaders and Protesters, The Future of Citizens' Organizations in Israel," in which he forecast the future of non-profit organizations in Israel. Among other things, he prepared a list of guidelines for donors in Israel and abroad. Eliezer advised the donors to not support projects that they would not support in another country, and to consult with an expert in community services to understand whether the project is indeed worth of their support. He also wrote that one must carefully examine the organization before donating, and he wrote, "Stay away from any program that should be a responsibility of the Israeli government, unless it is a demonstration project to catalyze government agencies into action."

He advised potential donors to choose innovative projects, to avoid projects that do not fit the evolving needs of Israel, and in general to follow the opinions of people in the field rather than bureaucrats.

"Always ask yourself what the influence of a particular project will be five or ten years hence. Are new policies or services likely to spin off from the effort? Or will it be just hit and run? For those who have already decided to donate to a particular project, he advised

that they demand periodic reports and professional evaluation of the project and, "Don't settle for photos of children or tear-jerker success stories...Do not get involved in raising money on an ongoing basis if you have no say on how it is spent .... Think of yourself as a partner in the project, not a casual benefactor."

He called on donors to be courageous and assertive and to not apologize for asking questions. "Remember that the worth of the cause you support cannot always be judged by the number or the status of the friends you make. On the contrary, you can sometimes judge success by listing the people you upset by your efforts."

As a proud Zionist, Eliezer concluded the booklet, which was intended primarily for donors from abroad, with a call to Diaspora Jews to immigrate to Israel.

"The ultimate form of participation in Israel's affairs is, of course, aliya, for people remain Israel's greatest need. Unfortunately, most American Jews are quite ambivalent in their attitudes on this subject. They glow with pride at the thought that an American immigrant's son gave his life while leading the Entebbe raid, yet aliya remains to them a conflict-ridden issue."

Eliezer called on the Jewish community federations in the U.S. to allocate some of the funds raised each year to support the practical needs of American immigrants in Israel, for "'making aliya' is not only a private act of the individual, but also a contribution by that individual's home community to the enrichment of the Jewish state." He concluded the booklet with the following sentence: "Immigration is still Israel's lifeblood, no matter how much money is raised for the UJA. "

Over the years, many donors have called Eliezer asking him to recommend charities to which they should donate. Eliezer would not give donors the names of specific NGOs but would advise them

to first look for those that have basic certifications, such as for proper management, and the approval of section 46 which grants an income tax credit for donations [in Israel]. Eliezer suggested that following these inquiries, donors call the organization directly and do their homework before donating to it. He admired donors who took their money seriously. When donors who came to Israel would call Eliezer to ask for advice, he would first ask them how long they would be there. If they said they were flying back that night, Eliezer would tell them that their attitude toward donating was not serious enough. He believed that a donor who wants to take his money seriously, must devote at least a few days to examine the organizations to which he is donating.

A few years after the publication of the book "Giving Wisely," Eliezer, together with psychologist Dr. Menachem Gottesman, established a private center to mediate between NGOs and potential donors. Called "The International Foundation Center," it was designed to advise individuals and small non-profits in the raising of money from Jewish foundations around the world. The center would assist those associations in submitting the necessary materials to donors, in formulating donation requests, and in providing budget proposals. Eliezer and Menachem recruited students who gathered information about Jewish foundations in the world that may donate to NGOs in Israel, and entered their details on a computer.

Another team of students was instructed by Eliezer on how to formulate the associations' requests for support from the foundations. Eliezer and Menachem traveled all over the country to get a closer look at the activities of the associations that requested their help, and to make sure that they were working properly and achieving significant results.

The associations paid The International Foundation Center a

small sum of money for the service provided to them, and if the association's proposal, formulated by the center, obtained a significant contribution from one of the funds, the payment for the service would increase accordingly. Dr. Gottesman talks about Eliezer's great thoroughness in preparing the proposals for the funds. "Eliezer read every request and was very meticulous in his wording. It was a great privilege to work with him."

Following the success of the center, Eliezer and Menachem decided to open a branch in Los Angeles to provide a similar service to small and medium-sized non-profit organizations from Israel who were operating there. Disastrously, it was discovered that the man appointed by them to run the office in Los Angeles embezzled funds collected from the charities. With great sorrow, Eliezer and Menachem were forced to close not only the branch they opened in the United States, but also the center they had established in Israel.

In 1996, Eliezer fulfilled another dream in the field of philanthropy. The School of Social Work at the Hebrew University created a chair for the study of volunteering and non-profit organizations. Eliezer, who researched, wrote, and dealt with the subject of volunteering, non-profits and philanthropy for many years, was chosen to head the new chair.

In the United States, universities had offered courses and degrees in non-profits and volunteering for many years. But until the mid-1990s, there was no academic institution in Israel that dealt with the subject. The new chair was established with the assistance of L. Jacques Ménard, a Catholic Canadian in his fifties, who was an investment advisor. During his business career, Ménard served as a board member for a number of nonprofits and showed great interest in volunteering.

He believed that the power of the business community should be

harnessed to solve social problems and, as a result, established the L. Jacque Ménard Chair in Social Work for the study of Volunteer and Nonprofit Organizations at the Hebrew University. Among the topics studied were fundraising methods, funding sources, election of a board of directors, financial control, legal status and by-laws of foundations, and more.

Professor Mona Khoury-Kassabri, who is currently the dean of the School of Social Work, studied philanthropy with Eliezer in those years. She took a course in which the students were required to assist in raising funds for one of the non-profits. She says that Eliezer was not only the course lecturer but was also a personal model to emulate and inspire. "The subject of philanthropy was for him not only a theoretical field of study which he knew in depth, but also a field in which he was personally active. He not only taught us the field, but also tried to convey to us his enthusiasm for practicing it, and it was very significant."

About ten years later, the Center for the Study of Civil Society and Philanthropy in Israel was established at the Hebrew University. It was founded and directed by Professor Hillel Schmid, whose doctorate Eliezer had supervised in the early 1980s. Eliezer was already retired when the center was established but he was appointed as one of the two chairmen of the center. Professor Schmid says that Eliezer encouraged the center's staff to conduct research in diverse fields. From time to time, Eliezer would also criticize certain things that in his opinion required correction, but would always do so in good spirits. Professor Schmid and the other staff members of the center had great respect for Eliezer as one of the pioneers of philanthropy research in Israel and one of the few who worked in the field before the center was established.

In the year 2000 Eliezer published an expanded second edition

of the guide "Giving Wisely."[13] For the first time, the guide was also published in Hebrew, and was addressed not only to donors from abroad but also to donors in Israel, and to citizens who were in need of donations or of the services of the NGOs. In the chapter, "A Resource Directory for Israelis" Eliezer wrote, "…the author hopes that 'Giving Wisely' will serve as a helpful, although partial handbook for Israeli professionals, clients and citizens who are in need of information about resources…Unfortunately, many Israelis have little knowledge about the wide range of non-profit services available to them or whom to contact in order to apply. There is a tremendous ongoing practical need by Israeli citizens and human service professionals for information about services and resources available from non-profit organizations."

The questionnaires that Eliezer sent to non-profit organizations for the new edition were similar to the questionnaires for the first edition, but he added various sections to them. Unlike the first edition, which included organizations only in the fields of health, education and welfare, the second edition included all kinds of non-profit organizations that provided services to the public. Eliezer made great efforts to ensure that all relevant organizations had an equal opportunity to appear in the book and to that end he published ads in all the large Israeli newspapers, for a number of weeks, describing the goal of the book. The ads called on the organizations that had not received the questionnaire to contact Eliezer so they could be included in the book.

The new edition, like the previous one, did not include associations of government and municipal ministries, as they do not provide a tax

---

13  https://eliezerjaffe.com/wp-content/uploads/2014/08/giving-wisely-B-e.pdf

exemption for donations. Synagogues were also not included in the book because they did not fit the definition of "service organizations," but synagogues that provided services to the public were included in the book. The book also did not include political parties, as they do not entitle donors from abroad to tax exemptions; it did not include trade unions because of their connection to political parties and their funding by state, municipal and government sources.

In the chapter "Partnership Philanthropy," Eliezer asked the donors to pay close attention in choosing the bodies to which they donate. "If you just want to feel good for having helped someone or some organization, one can 'feel good' by doling out dollar bills or [Israeli] shekels to as many people as possible. But the wise donor, who really wants to help, should feel a personal involvement and sense of partnership with the organization or people being helped." Eliezer suggested that those seeking a philanthropic partnership concentrate on a particular organization or area and support them for several years in order to leave their personal mark on them.

"The more involved you become, the more intelligently you will be able to understand issues and to help. And the more intelligent you become in your philanthropy, the sooner you will become a partner with thousands of Israelis who are trying to create a better society."

Simultaneously with the publication of the new edition of "Giving Wisely," Eliezer uploaded all the data collected to a new website he set up, also called "Giving Wisely." The site was established as a joint project with the Hebrew University's School of Social Work. In contrast to the printed guide, the online edition of "Giving Wisely" made it possible to update and make changes and additions to the profiles of associations and organizations at any time.

The site also contained links to the websites and e-mail addresses of the various associations, which allowed for immediate and direct

access to them. While working on the site, Eliezer contacted the Registrar of Associations at the Ministry of Interior and asked for his help with the project. They provided Eliezer with a CD with a list of all the associations registered in the ministry. Once online, the associations were invited to complete any information about them that was missing. At the time of its launch, the new website included details aboutalmost all 27,300 Israeli NGOs.

After publishing the guide on non-profits, Eliezer thought it was ironic that Israeli foundations required non-profits who ask them for funding to provide them with extensive information and evidence of reasonable and responsible management, while most funds themselves were shrouded in secrecy regarding procedures, budgets, expenses, management and decisions.

In order to also promote transparency in the world of funds and endowments, he published another book, about a year after the publication of the guide for non-profit organizations, called, "Sources for Funding, The Israel Foundation Directory."[14] In this book, Eliezer listed 3,000 profiles of funds and endowments operating in Israel and reviewed the growth of the fund sector and its development. Eliezer believed that private foundations have a very important role to play in improving Israeli society and in realizing the philanthropic potential and efforts of donors in Israel and abroad.

The foundations opened the door for philanthropists to fulfill their desires and their charitable wishes, and to create genuine partnerships with NGOs in Israel, without the need for intermediaries. Eliezer's guide helped Israel's non-profit organizations find sources of funding and get to know the working methods of private foundations.

---

14  Book-Sources-for-Funding-English-B-E.pdf (eliezerjaffe.com)

In addition, its goal was to encourage private donors in Israel and abroad to establish private funds to support Israeli NGOs, to encourage innovative projects, and to cultivate leadership in the field of self-help organizations. Eliezer also uploaded the information about the funds and endowments to the "Giving Wisely" website.

Eliezer claimed that a single central authority in Israel should be created that would be responsible for licensing and supervising all non-profit organizations. He believed that splitting responsibilities between the various authorities, such as the Ministry of Interior, the Ministry of Finance and the Ministry of Justice, was wasteful and inefficient. In his book "Sources for Funding, The Israel Foundation Directory," he wrote, "Each office operates independently with its own registrar, reporting and supervision procedures, staff, criteria, offices and operating expenses and this reality burdens and confuses the public."

After publishing the guides and creating the site, Eliezer felt that the next step should be for the state to take responsibility for his project. He believed that the pursuit of transparency in the world of non-profits should not be the responsibility of an academic and hoped that the actions he had initiated so far would encourage government bodies to take on sponsorship of his project.

In practice, Eliezer worked to establish the GuideStar Israel website, which would be part of the GuideStar International project, which aims to illuminate the activities of organizations, to enable better communication between organizations and donors, volunteers, and interested parties, and among the various organizations themselves. GuideStar International's information was comprised of tens of thousands of the annual reports of the organizations.

Disclosure of the reports as official information led the organizations to know that they were exposed to the public eye and that they

should act accordingly. GuideStar websites had already been operating in the United States and England, and Eliezer was convinced that the State of Israel should also set up a website with a similar model. The efforts bore fruit. In 2010, the GuideStar Israel website was established, and became the main source for information about non-profit associations and organizations in Israel. The site was established as a government venture in cross-sectoral collaboration. It is managed by the Ministry of Justice in cooperation with JDC Israel and is accompanied by a public advisory committee that includes various factions in the government, civil and business sectors.

Following the establishment of GuideStar Israel, Eliezer felt that his mission was complete and decided to close the site he had set up. "Now that we have fulfilled our mission, we are closing the chapter of 'Giving Wisely' with a sense of satisfaction," he concluded in a statement issued to the media. "For 11 years, we worked alone as a public service in building a model for distributing free information about the third sector and paved the way for the establishment of GuideStar Israel." Eliezer saw in the action he had initiated evidence that individuals and public organizations have the ability to promote and improve the third sector and philanthropy in Israel.

Eliezer saw philanthropic work as one of the most satisfying experiences, a basic experience of Jewish life and of the Jewish religion. "This is a craft that requires talent, humility and wisdom while combining the heart with the mind," he wrote in one of his articles. "It carries with it a huge personal responsibility that may bring pleasure and satisfaction to those who are willing to engage in it. Those who chose it as a profession, chose the best of professions."

The growth of the non-profit sector and the establishment of the Israeli market economy necessitated, in Eliezer's opinion, the creation of a new charter, a new agreement, and legislation in order

to create a real partnership between the government and the third sector. Eliezer believed that the tax laws should be changed, including increasing the tax exemption for donors from 35% to 50%, and exempting the associations from V.A.T. In general, he claimed that the conditions of the third sector should be compared with the conditions of the business sector and that there should be as many benefits as possible in the areas of taxation in order to make its activity easier. "After all, the government must decide what its real relationship will be with the third sector," Eliezer wrote. "It would be a shame if the sector were considered only a secondary tool by the central government that would be overseeing, directing and exploiting it. The healthier scenario is of a genuine partnership in which the administration encourages the third sector and private philanthropy through legislation for the growth of the sector."

## Chapter Thirteen

# The Israel Free Loan Association (IFLA) – "Ogen"[15]

In the early 1990s, large waves of immigrants from the Soviet Union and Ethiopia began to arrive in Israel. One day Eliezer brought his twin daughters, Naomi and Ruti, to a Jerusalem hotel near their home to see the new immigrants who lived there. At that moment, buses filled with new immigrants arrived straight from the airport. Eliezer said excitedly to his daughters: "Look, girls, this is exactly what *kibbutz galuyot*[16] looks like!" In the evening, when he returned home and saw the scenes of the arriving immigrants on the news, Eliezer began to think about how he could contribute to the national effort of absorbing them.

As one who believed that every citizen should be committed to social action, Eliezer invited some of his friends to join him in brainstorming about how they could help the immigrants. Eliezer was already aware that the absorption authorities in the country stopped taking care of immigrants a year after they arrived in Israel, at which

---

15 Today the name is "Ogen" which means "anchor" in Hebrew.

16 "Kibbutz galuyot" is the Hebrew term referring to the "ingathering of the exiles" that will occur during the Messianic period.

time they are expected to become "ordinary citizens". But he had learned from experience that even a year after arrival, immigrants will still not master the language, will still suffer from difficulties in earning a living and will probably not have enough ties with veteran Israelis who could help them. It was clear that the immigrants would need money to pay rent, to buy clothes or to start a business. The question that arose was: What would be the best way to help them with that?

True to his social philosophy, Eliezer did not think that the proper way to help immigrants was to buy furniture or clothing for them, but to provide them with a loan that would enable them to make their own decisions about what they would purchase. Eliezer drew inspiration for this concept from Maimonides' eight degrees of charity that appear in the laws of gifts to the poor: "A great virtue that has none above it, is when one holds the hand of a Jew who has fallen into poverty, and gives him a gift or a loan or enters into partnership with him or finds him work to strengthen his hand, until he no longer needs people and does not ask [for support], and it is said: 'And you hold him as though a stranger, a resident, and he shall live among you (Leviticus 25, 35), that is, hold him so that he does not fall and become in need.'"[17]

Maimonides points out that the highest level of charity is to give the needy a loan or a job that will allow him to help himself, maintain his dignity and become independent. Although the banks also allowed immigrants to take out loans, it was clear that they would have difficulty meeting the strict loan terms, and that they could get ensnarled in paying high interest rates on every loan they took out.

That was how the idea of the Israel Free Loan Association was

---

17   Maimonides Mishnah Torah, Laws of Gifts to the Poor, 10:7.

born -- an organization that would lend interest-free sums of money to immigrants. The economic plan was that when the loans were repaid to the association, they would be rolled over as loans to others. The idea of interest-free loans was not new. At the beginning of the 20th century, many charities were established in the United States that provided such loans, mainly for immigrants from Europe, for the purchase of homes and the establishment of new businesses. Eliezer decided to bring the idea to Israel.

In contrast to other local *g'machim*[18] that provided interest-free loans in small amounts, and were accessible only to small family and community circles, Eliezer sought to establish a large national body that would be managed professionally and transparently, and that would assist with significant sums of money to broad circles of borrowers.

In the beginning, the association was intended only for new immigrants from Ethiopia and the Soviet Union. Eliezer received the initial amount from two donors from New York who decided to celebrate their fortieth wedding anniversary by donating twenty thousand dollars to four Israelis who were working for the good of the public. Eliezer, who was known for his public activities in the Zahavi organization, was chosen by the couple as one of the four and he decided to invest the amount he received in the new association.

Shortly after its establishment, the association received another significant contribution, following an article published by Eliezer in the Jerusalem Post, in which he outlined the association's goals. A

---

18   "G'mach" is an acronym in Hebrew for *g'millut hassadim*, which can mean charity or acts of kindness. A "g'mach" can be not only for the loan of money, but also for the loan of clothing, housewares, or other objects.

few days after the article was published, while attending a conference in Boston, a Jew from Bloomington, Indiana called Eliezer. "I read your article in the newspaper," he told Eliezer, "and I would like to meet with you." A few days later, Eliezer met with him and left the meeting with a donation of one hundred thousand dollars. This propelled the organization to a whole new level.

Edward Cohen was another donor who came to Eliezer following the same article in the newspaper. Cohen, a native of Iraq who immigrated to Israel from England in the 1980s, had a family charitable foundation, and he would occasionally donate their money to new and intriguing initiatives. After reading about the new association in the newspaper, he met Eliezer and was captivated by his charms. As an accountant who came from the financial world and was a member of the London Stock Exchange, he liked the idea that the association's money was rolled over and over again and was thus used by many borrowers. He donated twenty thousand dollars to the association.

Surprised by Cohen's generosity, Eliezer invited him to join the new association's board of directors. In addition to Eliezer and Edward Cohen, the board of directors included Yona Cohen, who was treasurer of the Jerusalem branch of Zahavi, Yechiel Ozeri, a longtime friend of Eliezer and Rivka, and Miriam Jaffe, Eliezer's sister-in-law who lived in their neighborhood.

At the beginning of its journey, the association operated in a small room in the offices of the Jerusalem branch of the Zahavi association located on Metudela Street, not far from the Jaffe family home on Azza Road. The modest office had a table and several chairs. On one side of the table sat the immigrants who came to request a loan, and on the other side, two volunteers. It didn't take long before many immigrants flocked to the place, to receive loans of only a few hundred

dollars, to make it easier for them to adapt and integrate into Israel. If they came from far away, they also received a refund of the travel expense from the association.

In the beginning, the conditions set for obtaining a loan from the association were as follows: The applicant for the loan had to be a new immigrant, up to five years in the country. The loans, which were linked to the dollar exchange rate, ranged from $2,000 to $3,000 for a single applicant, or up to $15,000 for starting a business. In some cases, Eliezer and his association members showed flexibility and assisted immigrants with larger amounts. These cases were called "extraordinary operations" by members of the association. Among these operations were: assistance to an immigrant from Ethiopia who wanted to bring his mother's body to Israel for burial, assistance to parents of children with special needs in financing trips for their children, assistance to a family who immigrated from Italy and ran into major financial difficulties, and assistance to two immigrants, a husband and wife, who contracted AIDS.

Rumors of the new association spread by word of mouth. As time went on, more and more immigrants, with diverse needs, arrived at the association's small office to apply for the interest-free loans. The members of the association, led by Eliezer, began to raise additional donations that would allow them to provide loans to more people. As the circle of borrowers grew, a shortage of space developed.

One day, a Jew named Leeor Sabbah, from North Carolina in the United States, came to Israel, learned of the association's existence and asked to help. In his meeting with Eliezer at the Jerusalem hotel where he was staying, he asked to visit and see the association's offices.

Eliezer brought him to the little room in the Zahavi branch. Sabbah stayed there for about two hours and talked to the new immigrants

who came to apply for loans. On the way back to the hotel he said to Eliezer, "I was very impressed with everything you do and I want to set up my own fund within yours, but I do not understand how you are able to work like this, without a drop of privacy."

After all, in that room people could hear everything, and there was also quite a bit of crying. Eliezer told Sabbah that as a social worker he was well aware of the problem, but these were the conditions available to the association. Sabbah instructed Eliezer to find a suitable apartment in Jerusalem for the association's activities. "I will buy it," he said, "and you will pay me a low rent." Eliezer located a small three-room apartment, not far from his home, at 64 Azza Road. After it was purchased by a lawyer on Sabbah's behalf, Eliezer asked how much he had to pay for the rent. The answer he got from him was: one dollar a month, at the end of each year.

The association's move from Zahavi's offices to its new home had finally separated its activities from Zahavi's activities. Zahavi's activity waned during these years, until it ceased completely. Eventually, Zahavi's people decided to invest the remaining money in the association in establishing an interest-free loan fund for large families within the framework of the association founded by Eliezer. This decision was made without the involvement of Eliezer.

Before long, the association's activities expanded even further and the problem of overcrowding arose in its new home as well. The sixty square meters of the apartment could no longer accommodate the large number of people who frequented the place. In the apartment next to the association's new office lived a widower, a cancer patient, who was friendly with the association's staff. When he died, he granted in his will the first right of purchase of his apartment to the association. Eliezer returned to Leeor Sabbah and suggested that he purchase and connect the apartments and thus double the size of the office.

Sabbah granted the request, purchased the apartment, connected the apartments, and doubled the amount of rent to two dollars a month.

The association's activities within a residential building also had environmental implications. Some of the people who came to the association's offices would wait in the stairwell or in the garden of the building. The association's workers also received clients on a bench at the entrance to the building, in cases of disabled people who had difficulty reaching the second floor. Eliezer, who felt the need to show gratitude to the building's occupants for their tolerance of the association's activities, took over the management of the house committee and began to take care of the building. Among other things, he made sure that the stairwell was painted and the roof of the building was sealed against water. The tenants, for their part, appreciated Eliezer's work, and were happy for the association's activity in their building.

A few years after its establishment, the association began granting loans not only to new immigrants but also to senior citizens. The decision to make the interest-free loans available to a wider audience stemmed from the needs in the field. Five years after the association was founded, it had already provided five million dollars in loans to thousands of applicants. About two hundred loans were given on average each month. The main purposes for which the loans were granted were: assistance in purchasing an apartment or furniture for immigrants who left the caravans where they lived when they arrived in Israel, dental care, clothes for babies and children, water, electricity and phone bills, enrolment and tuition costs for higher education, and assistance to single-parent families, to large families and of course to new immigrants.

The association continued to grow for the next five years. Ten years after its founding, it had raised about ten million dollars. In

that decade the association distributed twenty-eight million dollars to fifteen thousand borrowers. As time went on, the categories for lending also expanded. The association began to provide loans for surrogacy and for the adoption of children abroad, and after the outbreak of the second intifada in 2000, it also provided loans to victims of terrorism and to business people who were economically affected by the security situation.

The seriousness of the economic reality in the country had doubled the number of applications to the association. If until the year 2000 the association approved about one hundred and fifty loans every month, after the outbreak of the intifada it began to approve more than 350 loans a month. The board of the association had also expanded over the years. A decade later, there were eleven members of the board, which was chaired by Eliezer.

In 2001, the association received a citation[19] from Minister Yuli Tamir, the Minister of Immigrant Absorption, for "its unique contribution of constructive economic assistance to immigrants while maintaining their dignity and self-confidence."

One of the departments that developed in the association over the years had been the area of small business loans. In the early years, it was mainly new immigrants who had difficulty raising money to start their own businesses. Although the association had not approved loans for businesses that had not yet been established, it certainly assisted with loans to existing businesses that had run into difficulties or needed an economic boost in order to take off.

One of the loans was given to two Ethiopian immigrants who decided to import into Israel the special flour used to make injera,

---

19  The name of the citation in Hebrew is *Magen Hasar* ("Shield of the Minister").

the Ethiopian bread. The couple went to Ethiopia to buy the flour but then the port in Ethiopia was shut down for about two months and the flour they purchased spoiled. The couple approached the association, and with the help of a loan they rebuilt the business.

In contrast to the stringent tests required by the state for eligibility for benefits, the association's policy, from its inception, was to not make it too onerous for the borrower to obtain a loan, but rather to examine his ability to repay it. In order to obtain a loan, the association required the borrower to present a pay slip or proof of other fixed income as well as to sign two guarantors who also had a fixed income. The amount of the monthly repayment of the loans was determined according to his financial ability. The basic principle was that the loan should be repaid according to the schedule set out in the agreement made with the borrower. The borrowers knew that the repayment of their loan was not only a debt imposed on them but it also enabled the association to help other people. The association showed flexibility towards borrowers who ran into difficulties and agreed to spread their repayments over a longer period. Only a few percent of the loans became "problem loans."

For those exceptional cases where borrowers ignored the repayment obligation, the association set up a legal department that dealt with debts, sometimes with the help of the courts and writs of execution if necessary. Eliezer always used to emphasize, both to the borrowers and to the members of the association, that the association's money does not belong to it but to the donors and therefore the association cannot afford to harm them. There have also been rare instances where the association waived reimbursement. One such case was when an Ethiopian couple who received a housing loan fell ill with AIDS and lost their jobs. Eliezer convened the association's board, which made an exception and waived the debt.

The percentage of borrowers whose loans were not repaid to the association was less than one percent over the years.

Loan applications rejected by the association were also revisited by members of the association's board. Yechiel Ozeri, who served as a member of the board for more than ten years, chaired an exceptions committee that held discussions on the loan applications that were rejected. "We carefully examined the applications," says Ozeri, "we asked questions, and despite the strict adherence to the criteria, there were also quite a few cases in which we found it appropriate to approve a loan anyway."

Eliezer himself was always careful to maintain the criteria for granting loans, but sometimes, on a personal level, he helped borrowers so that they could meet the criteria. Yona Cohen, who ran the association for 23 years, tells of the case of a woman in financial distress who asked to borrow two thousand dollars from the association but could not find two guarantors who would enable her to receive the loan. Eliezer did not compromise on the need for guarantors but generously agreed to be a guarantor for the woman. Eventually, she found it difficult to meet the loan repayments and Eliezer returned the amount from his own money.

As a rule, Eliezer always knew how to separate organizational and public policy from personal kindness. His adherence to clear rules and criteria in the management of the association did not contradict his desire to help every person. One day Eliezer met Yona Cohen on Azza Road and asked for her help. "A woman with a grey coat passed by," he told her, "and asked me for money to buy food for Shabbat. I did not have a significant amount in my pocket, so I went up to the house to bring her more money, and in the meantime she disappeared." Eliezer asked Yona to help him locate the woman to bring her more money.

In addition to being the founder and chairman of the association, Eliezer was also primarily responsible for raising donations for the association. In order to increase the number of donations, Eliezer suggested to donors that they create funds in their names or in the name of their family or friends, within the framework of the association, and the money would be returned to these funds when the loans were reimbursed, so that the donation was recycled again and again. The initial amount for setting up such a fund was NIS 35,000. The association provided the fund owners with a detailed semi-annual report on the condition of their loan fund, including the number of loans and the amounts that had been granted and repaid.

The owners of the personal and family funds also received information about the "help index" of their fund. The help index was a measure invented by Eliezer, which meant that the help provided by the foundation increased by a certain percentage.

If the fund's money has already been lent, returned to it and lent again, its help index was 200 percent, because instead of donating a dollar, the fund had actually donated two dollars, and so on. The more years the fund existed, the higher its help index became. Over the years, hundreds of such funds were established within the association.

One of the foundations was set up in the name of Edward Adler of New York who was killed at the age of 31 while he was helping a nurse who was attacked by an armed man. Adler's family received decorations of heroism for his brave deed but sought a way to perpetuate his memory in a way that expressed the character of their son, who loved to help others. The family contacted the association and asked to set up a loan fund in Edward's name. Within a few years, the fund provided loans with a total value of more than one

million shekels to dozens of small businesses in Israel and helped them overcome financial difficulties and prosper.

In many cases, the establishment of a single fund led to the establishment of several additional funds. This happened, for example, when a childless woman who read a newspaper article about the association asked to meet with Eliezer to consult with him about the distribution of her assets after her death. Eliezer met with the woman several times and after her death it was discovered that she had left a significant sum of money for the establishment of a fund in her name. The same woman had two sisters in the U.S. who adopted the fund their sister opened and donated money to it for every one of their grandchildren's birthdays. When one of the sisters became widowed, she opened an additional fund in memory of her husband, and the family began to donate to this fund, as well, every time there was a family event.

Steven and Faith Cohen, a couple from Ma'ale Adumim, learned about the fund of the childless woman from Eliezer, and they liked the idea. In honor of their 40th wedding anniversary, their children gave them the gift of establishing an interest-free fund in their name. They did it with contributions from friends and family, and throughout the years it has grown steadily thanks to additional amounts that the family continued to donate to mark family events. Through the association's recycling mechanism, the family's original donation funds were repaid five times in a few years, providing loans to more than one hundred different families.

In the spirit of "It is pleasant that he who demands [a good deed] also fulfills one," Eliezer himself established family funds in memory of his relatives, to which he donated. At first these were funds to commemorate Rivka's parents and his own relatives. He later set up a fund in memory of Rivka, his beloved wife, after her death. About

a year before his death, he changed the name of the fund to a "Fund in the name of Eliezer and Rivka Jaffe."

During one of the association's meetings, one of the employees suggested turning the funds into anonymous funds after a number of years. Eliezer objected. He explained that the commemoration of their loved ones was very important to donors and therefore it was important for them to be able to identify with the dedicated funds they had set up. In one case there was a donor who asked to remain anonymous. Since according to the association's bylaws, it was not permitted to establish an anonymous fund, Eliezer named the fund after Homer Simpson, the famous protagonist of a cartoon TV series.

Another idea of Eliezer's was to offer fund owners the opportunity to designate their funds for loans in a particular field. For example, a dedicated fund was set up to help families who wanted to adopt children from abroad, another fund helped single-parent families, and so on. Donors to whom educational issues were close to their hearts could choose to allocate their money to loans for education. Similarly, some donors allocated their funds for families of sick people.

One of Eliezer's most notable characteristics in all of his social endeavors was the identifying of needs that were not met in other frameworks. Every time he encountered such a need, he thought about how he could address it as part of his activity. When he discovered that the state helps people with disabilities to buy a car but does not help them buy accessories for such a car, he turned to donors who had a family member with a disability and suggested that they set up a fund to provide loans to parents of children with special needs that, in addition to aiding with other things, would also help buy necessary accessories for these special cars. According to the policy of the Ministry of Welfare, a child with a disability who is

being raised in his home receives less government assistance than the amount that institutions and hospitals would receive for him, if he were living there.

Eliezer, in all the welfare issues of children and youth, saw the importance of parents raising their children at home and not in an institution. He believed that the quality of life of children with disabilities improves considerably when they grow up in the home of their parents so he did his best, also within the association, to financially help the parents who chose to raise their children at home.

Shirley and Naftali Solvey came across a news item in the Karmiel local newspaper about Shai, a one-and-a-half-year-old baby with cerebral palsy, whose parents had abandoned him at the hospital due to his disability. The newspaper and the hospital issued a moving plea to the public to find Shai a warm and loving home. The couple, who were blessed with five children of their own, decided this was their chance to help a child on whom fate had not smiled. When they saw Shai, their eyes sparkled, and when they first hugged him, they realized they had a new baby in the family. From the moment they adopted Shai, the Solvey couple believed in his ability to improve and develop and wanted to give him all the resources to succeed.

Over the years, they were assisted three times by the association. They received interest-free loans to finance surgeries and equipment that were critical to Shai's development. Once they used a loan to buy a special walking belt, a treadmill and a special brace for Shai, another time they took out a loan to buy a special tricycle and another time to buy a saxophone. Shai progressed beyond all expectations. He completed a special program for volunteers in the IDF and at the same time began working at a post office in Karmiel.

Another story was that of Yosef, the youngest child of Esther Yaakobi, a single mother of three. Yosef was a severely disabled child

with autism. Although Esther worked throughout her years of raising Yosef, she found it difficult to take care of all her son's needs on her own. She decided to apply to the association for a loan so that she could adapt her home to Yosef's needs. For 16 years Esther lived on the third floor of a building without an elevator. At one point she felt she could no longer bear the burden. She turned to several places with requests to help her fund the move to another apartment but to no avail. Esther turned to the association and received assistance from a fund set up by the Sabbah family; it had been created with the aim of helping people who work but are experiencing financial difficulties. Thanks to that Sabbah fund, Esther and many other borrowers were able to sustain themselves with dignity and start a new chapter in their lives.

The September 11, 2001 attacks created an economic crisis in the United States and caused economic losses to Leeor Sabbah, the donor who financed the association's offices on Azza Road. Eliezer decided to sell the apartments and return the money to Sabbah. The association began to look for a new home in Jerusalem and found one in the Talpiot neighborhood, in a complex that was used in the past for sanitary fixtures.

Eliezer travelled abroad again and raised funds for the purchase of the complex. In 2008, the association moved from Azza Road to 29 Rivka Street in the Talpiot neighborhood. In this move there was also the closing of a personal circle, as it was a short distance from where Eliezer began his work as a social worker at the Talpiot transit camp in 1957, and now he established, in the same neighborhood, the largest social enterprise he created in the course of his life. The new and spacious offices enabled the association's employees and volunteers to provide the many clients with a more dignified, pleasant and discreet environment.

The association's administrative expenses were financed in a number of ways. There were donations dedicated to cover its overhead expenses. In addition, the interest accrued on deposits in the association's bank accounts was used to cover costs until the next loan was made. The association also charged modest management fees from the funds it managed and the borrowers also paid a small, one-time management fee when their loan was approved. Eliezer personally took meticulous care of the association's money.

He paid for his fundraising flights for the association from his study fund at the university, and he insisted on covering the expenses incurred, during his time abroad, from his own pocket. The board members begged him to accept reimbursement for the money he spent on his activities for the benefit of the association, but managed to persuade him only partially and for a certain period. When he had already agreed to receive reimbursement of expenses, he made sure that everything was recorded in detail in the minutes of the board meetings.

Over the years, the association's board expanded. When it was established, it had only seven members, as required by law. The board gradually expanded to thirteen members. The way more members were added was through a recommendation from one of the board members and a preliminary discussion of the board on the recommendation. Each new member served as a board member for a six-month probationary period, after which board members decided whether to add him as a full-time permanent member. In this way, Uri Jaffe, Eliezer's son, and Ohad Eini, his son-in-law, were also added. In addition to the permanent members of the board, Eliezer saw the importance of involving external consultants and employees of the association who were not members of the board, in order to enrich the discussions.

Events in Israel through the years led the association to open additional channels for interest-free loans. In 2005, the State of Israel uprooted 8,600 residents from 21 settlements in Gush Katif. Although the state compensated the families for their homes,[20] many of the evacuees lost their livelihoods following the displacement and some used the compensation money for daily subsistence. The association offered the evacuees help, and many accepted the offer and received loans.

A year later, in the summer of 2006, the Second Lebanon War broke out and severely damaged the northern settlements. The state provided compensation to those whose homes or businesses were damaged, but many residents needed financial support to recover from the damage of the war. The association rallied to help them. With the aid of donors from abroad, who donated about a million dollars to the association, a special fund was established for business owners affected by the war in the North and a loan of $15,000 was offered to each. The amount was the same as that for business owners during non-war times. The difference was reflected in the benefits and concessions given to the victims of the war.

In regular times the association approved interest-free loans linked to the dollar exchange rate, but business owners in areas that had suffered from bombings were exempted from this linkage. In regular times, the association required business owners to have four or five guarantors and required a business plan. Business owners in the bombed-out areas were required to bring only two guarantors and were not required to submit a business plan.

---

20  It was a long and onerous bureaucratic process and in many cases the families felt they did not receive amounts that reflected what they had lost.

During the war in the North, the association provided residents with greater financial aid than that provided by government ministries. When Eliezer was asked if he did not think the association was performing roles that the government should be doing, he replied that in his view the government cannot do everything and should not do everything, and sometimes when it tries to do everything, it does not do it well. As a social activist throughout his life, Eliezer believed that even in a country with a social policy, citizens cannot evade taking action, and must be involved alongside the government in repairing society.

At one point, the association's people, on the advice of Edward Cohen, decided to switch from dollar loans to shekel loans. This was due to the rise in the value of the dollar which caused the borrowers to repay a higher amount than they received. After the decision was made, the shekel began to grow stronger for a long time period of time. In retrospect, the decision prevented the association from taking a significant financial loss.

Bob and Trudy Gottesman of New York were among the major donors to the association for years and helped thousands of families rebuild their lives. Bob Gottesman found in the association's philanthropic model an effective method of donating to charity and helping others. He particularly liked the fact that the donation funds are repeatedly used to give monthly loans, thanks to the repayment funds of previous loans. He saw the contribution to the association as a kind of permanent benefit that helps low-wage workers "finish the month" [debt-free]. In 2010 Gottesman funded a national campaign of the association, the first of its kind since it was founded twenty years earlier. The ads were intended to inform the general public about the existence of interest-free loans. They were broadcast on local radio stations for over ten days and the results were not long

in coming. The campaign increased the number of applicants to the association tenfold and significantly helped to expand the range of applicants seeking assistance from the association.

At the end of the public campaign, the Gottesmans decided to make a contribution to the association in the amount of one million dollars. Eliezer congratulated the couple on the donation itself but no less on their deep and long-standing partnership with the association. In a statement to the media, he emphasized that although the Gottesman couple's contribution would significantly increase the association's ability to provide assistance to the needy, the organization was still far from being able to meet the needs of all those in Israel who need this type of assistance. "Unfortunately, we can only help a tiny fraction of those who need our help in the country and many others are left behind and serve as easy prey for credit sharks and the grey market, providing them with loans at exorbitant rates and condemning them to an endless cycle of distress and poverty."

In the six months following the association's advertising campaign, four thousand people approached it. Instead of 300 inquiries a month, the association's members began to deal with 600 inquiries. As a result of doubling the number of referrals in such a short time, the association had to freeze its activities for a short period. The significant increase in loan applications came after the association's decision to raise the amounts of loans to small businesses, and both of these factors led to the association's account simply being emptied. For several months the association was forced to approve loans only in accordance with the cash flow of the loan repayments already provided. Following the depletion of the association's funds, the board decided to reduce the loan amounts so that they could help a larger amount of loan applicants.

In 2011, twenty-one years after its establishment, eleven salaried

employees worked for the association and about twenty people volunteered for it.

From a small association with a sum of $20,000 which provided loans in small amounts to immigrants only, the association has over the years become "Ogen"[21] ("Anchor" in Hebrew) - a social finance group comprised of multiple non-profit organizations that provide credit, guidance and mentoring to families, individuals, small businesses and non-profits.

Ogen's loan funds amount to about NIS 500 million. So far, the organization has provided about 70,000 loans in the amount of NIS 1.5 billion and less than one percent of borrowers have been unable to repay their loans. In 2020, Ogen assisted approximately 3,500 victims of the coronavirus crisis and that year provided NIS 160 million in credit, 2.5 times more than in 2019.

Eliezer's vision came true, but of course he did not think, even for a moment, to rest on his laurels.

---

21   The story of how the name came to be changed appears in Chapter 15.

## Chapter Fourteen

## Looking to the Future

In the year 2000 Eliezer turned 67 years old. After 40 years of teaching in Hebrew University, with a rich variety of studies and thousands of students to his credit, he retired. At the same time, he continued to be Professor Emeritus in the faculty of Social Work and also the co-chairman of "The Center for the Study of Civil Society and Philanthropy in Israel." Outside of the academic world, in the social field, Eliezer continued to be vigorously active. He divided his time between Ogen and promoting the world of philanthropy and non-profits in Israel.

Due to the reputation that Eliezer had acquired in the field of non-profits, many people involved in the field came to him for advice. When someone would come to Eliezer and tell him that he wanted to start a new organization that would deal with a certain issue, the first question that Eliezer asked him was whether there was already an existing organization doing similar things. If the answer was yes, Eliezer suggested that person join the already existing association and work with it, instead of setting up a new one. Eliezer believed in collaborations, but more than that, he did not believe in setting up unnecessary associations whose activities did not meet a real need. If the initiative was innovative, Eliezer would

go to the next step, and try to understand the person, to determine how serious he was and how passionate he was about bringing his ideas to fruition.

He would check if the person already had the initial capital that would enable him to start operating, or the means to obtain such capital, and he would ask the social entrepreneur who will be the board members of the new association and whether he has already read the Amutot (Non-profits) Law and knew what the requirements were for proper management of an association. In many cases, Eliezer suggested to the person that he first establish a social business and not a non-profit. He believed that if a person can not only provide a certain service but also make a livelihood from it, that is the better route to follow.

One of the many who turned to Eliezer was Tova Hametz. Tova immigrated to Israel from the United States in 2001 as a young woman and tried to integrate into the world of social non-profits.

In 2006, she wanted to do a study about the non-profits that were active in the area of education, and when she heard about Eliezer and his in-depth knowledge of the third sector, she sent him an email in which she requested a meeting with him. She was surprised to receive a reply within half an hour in which Eliezer invited her to a meeting which lasted more than two hours. Tova shared with Eliezer her attempts to operate in the third sector, and he listened to her patiently. In the end he told her: "Any significant social initiative should not be dependent on you and should be able to exist after you. Since the one who initiates does not have to be at the center, every social initiative must be built from the beginning so that it will survive even without the initiator."

Tova, who was very impressed with Eliezer, wanted to learn more from him and offered her help in improving the website he set up

– "Giving Wisely." At first, she did so voluntarily, until Eliezer insisted on paying her. When he asked at what amount she evaluates the time she spends improving the site, she replied that she does not need to be paid at all. Eliezer replied that if she does not value her time, others would also not appreciate her time or her work. For two years, Tova worked in various jobs related to Eliezer's projects, in the field for various associations and in Ogen.

One of Tova's roles in Ogen was writing reports for donors. In this role she became aware of the power of Ogen's loan cycle, which was defined by Eliezer as "the help value." (Also called, "the help index.") A donor whose donation became a loan to three different people, one after the other, received a help index of 300%. Eliezer explained to Tova that one of the important rules in fundraising for non-profits was giving donors the feeling that the non-profit gave him, the donor, an excellent opportunity to be a benefactor. Eliezer believed that people, by their nature, want to give. One only needs to give them the opportunity to do so.

When the government website of GuideStar Israel was established, Eliezer decided to provide the new website with all the information collected on the "Giving Wisely" website. Tova, who invested heavily in promoting Eliezer's website and in entering the data of all the non-profits, initially objected to the fact that Eliezer provided the GuideStar website with all the data collected without requesting anything in return. Eliezer explained that his entire purpose in establishing the "Giving Wisely" website was to bring GuideStar to Israel, in the belief that the website would be able to promote transparency in the world of non-profit organizations in the best possible way. "There is no point in keeping the information we have if the public is not exposed to it," Eliezer said. "Our whole purpose was for the public good, and now the public good is that we will transfer all the

information to the new site." This was another important lesson that Tova received from Eliezer regarding the third sector, a lesson on the importance of information sharing.

In 2009, Tova stopped working for Eliezer and joined an initiative that entailed fundraising for non-profits through a website. There, too, she continued to seek Eliezer's advice. "There was no professional and sometimes personal decision, in the partnerships and projects I did, that I made without consulting Eliezer. Even in the two years I worked on another venture, I relied on him for all guidance and advice and he would always devote time to me. He never told me he was tired, busy, or feeling unwell, but always answered all my requests happily." Even when she left the world of non-profit organizations and started a business, Tova received encouragement and guidance from Eliezer. For Tova, Eliezer was her teacher and mentor for nearly a decade.

Rabbi Benny Lau, rabbi of the Kehillat Ramban Synagogue in Jerusalem, was assisted by Eliezer while caring for one of the families in his community who experienced economic collapse. Eliezer helped the family and in the course of his working with the family, he also introduced Rabbi Lau to the dark world of loans taken in the grey market. Rabbi Lau subsequently decided that there is no justification for every synagogue community to manage its own loan g'mach when there can be so many dangers in the field. He closed the loan fund of his synagogue and transferred all the money to Ogen.

A significant portion of the inquiries that reached Eliezer were about fundraising. As a researcher of the third sector and non-profit organizations and as the founder of a successful non-profit organization such as Ogen, Eliezer had gained an exemplary reputation in the field of resource mobilization. Eliezer believed that fundraising is a

profession that requires knowledge and skills and that an association that wants to survive and develop must specialize in these areas.

He used to say that there is a lot of philanthropic money in the world. Donors want to donate, the non-profits want to receive, and one just needs to create the connection between the two parties. To the directors of non-profit organizations who approached him for advice in the area of fundraising, Eliezer told them that they needed to be involved in the field of fundraising even if the organization had an official fundraiser. Eliezer believed that the fundraiser was only a representative of the association and that the best people to market the association were its board members.

One day the executive director of a non-profit came to Eliezer and asked him for advice on fundraising. Before answering in the affirmative, Eliezer asked the director: "Suppose a donor from New York wants to donate half a million dollars to your association tomorrow and he asks you how he can transfer the donation and get a tax exemption in New York. What will you tell him?" The embarrassed director did not know what to answer. Eliezer told him that a director who does not know how to answer basic fundraising questions, cannot entrust this important area to someone outside the organization.

One of the people who was greatly helped by Eliezer in learning the principles of fundraising was Benni Gur, who founded the "Mesimot" organization, which provides advice, training and coaching in the areas of fund-raising and public relations to directors of non-profits. In the early 1980s, Gur was the aliya *shaliah*, stationed in Cleveland, in his role as director of the Midwest Region of the aliya department of the Jewish Agency. He and his young family were adopted by Miriam Jaffe, Eliezer's sister-in-law.

When he returned to Israel, Gur served as Deputy General

Manager of the Jerusalem College of Technology (Machon Lev) in Jerusalem. His acquaintance in Cleveland with the Jaffe family led him to consult with Eliezer on fundraising for the college. In addition to the personal and deep bond formed between the two, Eliezer changed Gur's worldview in relation to the field of philanthropy. "Eliezer taught me that fundraising is not 'shnorring' but strategic work related to the marketing of values, and to the social connection of people to value-based ideas. I learned from him that the financial contribution is not a value in itself but expresses the social and value connection created between the donor and the organization. This is an ideological covenant created between both sides and not just an act of giving money. There is a reason his book is called, 'Giving Wisely.' Eliezer talked about the kind of giving where the donor is willing to give on his own and money is not taken from him through manipulations. In addition, he talked about intelligence in managing the fundraising system, which he sees as a strategic system that combines marketing, sales, advertising and persuasion. These are the elements that must be intelligently integrated in order to create motivation to transform taking to giving."

Eliezer, according to Gur, held the view that fundraising is a means of organizational and community empowerment. Giving people the opportunity to volunteer and be involved in fundraising for a particular organization strengthens their deep connection. "This is not just a job of technically raising money but a process that connects people to an organization through actions, experiences, challenges and shared goals." Gur later replaced Eliezer at the School of Social Work by teaching a course on Fundraising for Welfare Organizations. Teaching the subject at the university led Gur to delve deeper into the field of fundraising and to develop a course on the subject for the Israeli Center for Management, which prepares managers

for the social sector. Gur invited Eliezer to be a guest lecturer in the course. "Eliezer would come to the course with an academic aura, a pleasant personality and a new approach to resource mobilization and that had a tremendous magnetic force."

At one point, Gur turned the content of one of the courses into a digital kit. The kit included a videotaped interview with Eliezer on a number of key issues regarding resource mobilization. "Donors want to donate, the charities want to serve, and the trick is to connect them so that one can reach the other," Eliezer said in the same interview. "These are the most beautiful things that happen quietly but the work is tremendous and fruitful and contributes to the State of Israel in a fantastic way. We are talking about a huge amount of capital. There are billions of dollars that are given and whoever knows how to work in this area can absolutely obtain many resources for the organization that sends him. Organizations that don't understand the importance of learning how to work in a professional way in fundraising end up working in a wasteful way and with a lack of knowledge, and I feel sad seeing this. An organization that wants to survive must learn how to raise funds professionally."

Another person who assisted Eliezer in those years in the third sector was the economist Aharon Mor, who today works in the Ministry of Senior Citizens (today called the Ministry for Social Equality) where he is in charge of restoring Jewish rights and property. Mor studied for a master's degree in public administration and public policy and, as a former tax inspector, decided to write a thesis on the tax benefits provided to donors to non-profit organizations in Israel under section 46 of the Income Tax Ordinance. When he was looking for a mentor, everyone sent him to Eliezer.

Although he was very busy at the time, Eliezer agreed to mentor Mor. When he finished writing the thesis, Mor was asked to present

it at a conference for third sector organizations. Since he was on *shlihut* in Australia at the time, he asked Eliezer to present the work at the conference in his place. Eliezer agreed and did so while heaping much praise on Mor for his work. People at the conference later told Mor that they had never heard a professor praise his student in this way. Eliezer and Aharon later published a joint article on the issue of tax rebates for donors and its implications for fundraising in the third sector.

In 2001, the Hebrew University School of Social Work awarded Eliezer the Baerwald Medal. The award commemorates the name of Paul Baerwald, after whom the school is named. It was awarded to Eliezer for his many years of contribution to the development of the School of Social Work, for his actions to promote education for the social work profession, and for his work to develop welfare and philanthropy services in Israel. The reasons the award committee stated for giving him the award were that Eliezer played a key role in the development of social advocacy for vulnerable groups and for those who suffered from exclusion in society, and in promoting community organization for the empowerment of those groups.

His activity for changing social policy and his ability to integrate the needs of the field with academia was noted: "Professor Jaffe was and remains aware of social hardships and devotes much of his work to the study of equal rights and ways of dealing with poverty and underdevelopment. Principles of social justice and morality have guided and continue to guide him throughout his years of work and he is dedicated to imparting these values to his many students."

This was not the first award Eliezer received. Five years earlier, he had received from President Ezer Weizman the "Presidential Volunteer Medal" for the year 5756 (1995-6) in the field of family and community. Among the reasons stated by the award committee,

at whose helm stood Supreme Court Justice Dov Levin (Retired), were: "The Israel Free Loan Association is the jewel in the crown of Professor Jaffe's many years of public activity and volunteering. He spends many hours in the course of his busy day directing the association and recruiting donors. To accomplish this, he is assisted by a small staff of dedicated financiers and volunteers."

In 2004, Eliezer received the Sderot Conference Award for Contribution to Israeli Society, which was awarded to him at the conference's closing event. The award committee wrote that the award was given to Eliezer for his many years of contribution and activity in promoting societal security in Israel, and for being a unique example of a person who combined fruitful academic work as a teacher and researcher, with active personal social involvement for the betterment of Israeli society. "His personal activity as a volunteer is accompanied by activities to encourage volunteering and giving for various social goals. He has always looked deeply [into the issues], beyond the clichés of philanthropy, and he knew how to reach the deep roots of charity in order to motivate society to volunteer and recognize the power of involvement to drive social change for the good of the individual and the community."

In the spring of 2007, a cancerous growth was discovered in Rivka's head. Eliezer, the children, and the children-in-law were mobilized to care for Rivka and to make it easier for her. Eliezer devoted himself to his wife's care and refused to be aided by a foreign helper. Throughout Rivka's illness he was meticulous about guarding her sense of self-respect, modesty and privacy, despite the physical and mental difficulties she endured. Yael, a physician by profession, used her professional abilities and helped provide her mother with medical care.

During the early stages of the illness, she helped with the

determination and acceleration of essential tests, and in getting fast and efficient medical treatment from the best possible doctors. Going forward, she took care of adjusting medications, and also administered shots to her mother as needed. At one point Eliezer said to his daughter, "You should be your mother's daughter, not her doctor," and decided to move Rivka into a hospital setting. Yael talks with gratitude how her father discerned, without words, her need to be with her mother in song, hugs and experience and not as a professional caregiver.

Toward the end of her illness, Rivka was hospitalized at the hospice of Hadassah Hospital on Mount Scopus. On her first night in the hospital, Eliezer brought a folding bed and prepared to sleep next to her. This natural act on his part set a high human standard and as a result the children decided not to move from their mother's bedside throughout the period of hospitalization and shared shifts between them around the clock. They decorated her room with pictures, sat by her bed, recited psalms and prayers with her, talked to her and also played music and sang. Occasionally Rivka quietly joined in and sang with them. In the last months of her severe illness, Rivka was careful to recite the blessing "Blessed are you, O Lord, our God, the King of the universe, by Whose word all came to be." This blessing opened a small window to her deep faith and to her approach to her serious illness.

After about a month and a half in the hospice, on Elul 4, 5768, Tuesday, September 3, 2008, Rivka Jaffe died of cancer surrounded by all her loving family members. Heavy mourning fell on Eliezer and the children. In his eulogy to his beloved wife, Eliezer said, "In an attempt to summarize the main values of Rivka, I would include: deep love and boundless loyalty to the family and to the lives of the immediate and the extended family, the desire to help others

without seeking honor, strong faith in religion and Judaism, faith in the importance of education and self-education at all stages of life, and love of the Land of Israel and the people of Israel.

"I personally look at life as a short-term loan that we will all have to repay one day. This loan has to pay interest and the interest is 'good deeds' or 'fixing the world,' meaning leaving the world a little better than it was when we arrived here. Rivka returned a lot, a lot of 'interest' - good deeds, and she used her life in a most excellent and successful way. She was an excellent example for others. Throughout the years, and especially during Rivka's illness, she and I had the very special experience and joy of receiving pure love from our children, their spouses and our grandchildren – we witnessed the exemplary action of 'honoring one's mother and father.' The character of the children, most of it inherited from her, proves that Rivka has not really left us. The memories, values, education, habits, qualities, calmness and warm personality -- will accompany us all our lives and for generations. "

Many visitors came to the Jaffe family home during the days of shiva for Rivka. Among them was Harriet Hass, a niece of Alice, Eliezer's older sister. When she immigrated to Israel alone in 1979, Eliezer and Rivka adopted her as a daughter, often hosted her at their home, and helped her to become acclimated to the country and into the field of social work. As someone who lost her mother as a child, Hass found in Rivka the mother figure she was missing. When she married and had children, Rivka came to help her in the first days after each birth. For many years she cherished Eliezer and Rebecca for the hospitality and great kindness they bestowed on her.

During the days of the shiva, Eliezer told the many people who came to comfort them about Rivka's character and work, and spoke little about the period of her illness. At night, when the house was

emptied of comforters, he said to his children: "We are talking about the rich life of a mother and not about her death." Eliezer taught his children that many of the comforters tend to ask about a person's death and about his last moments. It is possible that this matter stems from a natural fear of death and a desire to control it. But what matters more is what one did in his life.

Eliezer's focus on life and strength was also evident after the days of the shiva were over when he said to his children: "If God forbid I get sick like Mother, put me in a hospice and go see a film at the cinema ..." He said things in a similar vein when they went up to visit Rivka's grave on Har HaMenuchot. "Go up to my grave in good weather and at a convenient time, and enjoy the view ...".

Eight days after Rivka's death, a bat mitzva party was held for Avital Lieberman, Ruth's daughter and the granddaughter of Yitz and Miriam Jaffe. Eliezer, who treated Yitz's grandchildren as his grandchildren, came to the bat mitzva party, even though he had only risen from shiva the day before. He brought Avital a piece of jewelry and wrote her a greeting in his name and in the name of Rivka. Avital, who related to Eliezer as to a grandfather, greatly appreciated the effort he made for her. Miriam, his sister-in-law, later said: "Eliezer was special to us all in many ways. We were warmed and absorbed his radiant light. I will always remember with gratitude and appreciation the fact that he filled a void for my children, due to the absence of their father, Yitz, his brother. He influenced their lives and was precious to them. This memory lives with me, with my children and with my grandchildren who were privileged to know him."

Eliezer continued his activities in the association and his other social enterprises, including the management of the house committee, together with his sister-in-law Miriam, even after the death of

Rivka. He did not change his lifestyle, but for the first time purchased a large TV and placed it in the living room of the house, a step that Rivka had objected to, and began to watch more movies, especially in the evenings. When his daughter asked him how he copes with loneliness, he replied, "I'm busy being busy."

Eliezer and Rivka had a subscription to the Jerusalem Theater. After Rivka's death, Eliezer gave the subscription to a cleaner who worked at his home. The cleaner, an immigrant from the former Soviet Union, was very moved by the gesture and by the gift itself.

When Rivka was alive, she used to prepare meals for Eliezer to take with him whenever he went to spend long hours in the association's offices in the Talpiot neighborhood. After her death, Yona Cohen, the association's veteran director, made sure that Eliezer did not forget to eat and continued Rivka's tradition. She shared with his children, more than once, that she scheduled lunch meetings, in order to arrange a meal for him.

Eliezer continued to live in the same apartment at 37 Azza Road, but began traveling more to be with his married children on Shabbat - Ruti and Yael in Jerusalem, Naomi in Elazar and Uri in Hashmonaim. For every such Shabbat he would make sure to arrive with a bouquet of flowers. His children and grandchildren remember with longing the bouquet that would peek in at the door of their house on Fridays, shortly before Shabbat, and behind it their father's smiling face.

Chen Jaffe, Eliezer's granddaughter, talks about the Shabbatot her grandfather spent in her family's home: "Saba (Grandpa) used to arrive just moments before Shabbat, wearing a white shirt slightly too big for him, ready to go out for the evening prayer. He always brought a bouquet of flowers that reminded him and us of our beloved grandmother Rivka, who loved anemones. On his return from

the synagogue, he would start singing the song 'Shalom Aleichem' in a melody that reminded me of Jerusalem. At dinner he would always express his astonishment at the amount of food that Mother prepared, and always claimed that we are piling up too much on his plate, and would not agree to finish the meal before reading a d'var Torah from the book "Nefesh Chaya" (In Hebrew: "The Living Soul"), which he had bought for us. (It is a book about the portion of the week that a friend of his – Yisrael Brody – wrote in memory of his wife Chaya.)

"In the course of Shabbat he would always ask every one of us about our achievements and our progress in our various areas [of study or work] and he was very proud of us. After Shabbat, Saba Eliezer would have a supper that included an omelet with ketchup and a few (if any) vegetables that we managed to persuade him to eat. With the short sentence of "Okey dokey" and "Have a good week" he would leave us and drive his white Mazda, smelling of peppermint, back to his home in Jerusalem."

Ohad Eini shares that as a service included in the experience of hosting Eliezer in their home, he sometimes offered to cut his hair. When he would agree (almost always, happily) he would reply to Ohad with compliments and admiration: "Just like a professional barber, and much cheaper!"

As a curious man who always took an interest in others, Eliezer began to be known to the people in his children's communities. In every community there were people who spoke to him and enjoyed his wisdom. Shira Rosenberg, a resident of Elazar and a childhood friend of Naomi and Ruti, relates that Eliezer was interested in her doctoral dissertation and encouraged her to continue, despite various delays. She mentioned his name in the dedication she wrote to her work. Another resident said that, during one of Eliezer's visits

to the synagogue, he said to his young son: "Look at this man. This is what a righteous man looks like."

On the notes he attached to the gifts he brought to his grandchildren, Eliezer continued to write: "Saba and Savta", even after Rivka's death. He told his children at one of the family events that he was trying to fill a little of the void left by Rivka, who took care of them and had taken a keen interest in their well-being, but admitted that he was not always successful. Eliezer also made sure to keep in touch with Rivka's siblings and to attend all their family's joyful occasions.

On Shabbatot when he stayed at home, Eliezer had some of the meals with his sister-in-law Miriam, Yitz's wife, who lived on the floor above him. Eliezer felt a deep family feeling towards Miriam, and even when it was suggested that he move into a more accessible home, he ruled out the possibility because he did not want to leave Miriam without her good neighbor.

One evening, about a year after Rivka's death, Eliezer told his son-in-law Ohad Eini that he had been invited to lecture at four different conferences in the U.S. and Canada, but there was a three-week gap between the conferences, and he was debating how to fill it. Ohad suggested that he join Eliezer and spend the time with him in between the conferences. At first Eliezer refused. "What will you do with an old man like me?" he said to Ohad, but Ohad insisted and managed to convince Eliezer. In October, 2009, Eliezer and Ohad traveled for three weeks of lectures and trips in Canada and the U.S. Ohad, who financed his own trip, was impressed by the fact that Eliezer, who financed the trip from his study fund, chose to stay in very modest accommodations throughout the trip. This conduct of Eliezer characterized all his travels abroad. Another thing that impressed Ohad was Eliezer's interest in people everywhere they went.

In Manhattan, New York, Eliezer and Ohad visited a synagogue

that operated near Mount Sinai Hospital, that also served as a sleeping space for homeless people and that had a soup kitchen. Eliezer sat down to eat with the residents of the place to talk to them and to hear their personal stories.

When they arrived at a large gambling site in the city of Las Vegas, Nevada, Eliezer sat down with dealers to interview them about their lives. Eliezer told Ohad during their trip that of all the wonderful and amazing things he saw in the world, he found that humans are the most amazing. "You should be curious and interested in the people around you," Eliezer said. "You should learn about the place from the locals, ask people about their occupation and not be embarrassed to develop a conversation with them, that is the way to meet a fascinating world."

Eliezer also took advantage of the trip for family visits. In Toronto, Canada, he visited his cousin Elka and his granddaughter Hadar Jaffe, who was in town for a year of National Service. In New York, too, he visited distant family members. He always believed, and thus told Ohad during their journey, that family has a supreme value. "One must not give up contact with family members, even with the most distant."

Another typical thing Eliezer did during the trip with Ohad was to try to recruit more friends and donors to Ogen. In addition to a visit with Bob and Trudy Gottesman, one of the association's major donors, while they were in New York, Eliezer met in Montreal, Canada, with people who wanted to hear about the association's activities. At the beginning of the meeting, Eliezer clarified that for him it was not a business meeting and that he had no intention of leaving the meeting with donations, but only to talk about the association and the social ideas behind its activities. For Ohad it was another opportunity to discover the secret of Eliezer's charm in his

philanthropic activities. "The people we met did not see Eliezer as someone who came to raise money but to make real personal contact with them. Wealthy people have a fear that others will love them only because of their money but with Eliezer you could always feel and know that he is really interested in you, not your money."

In March, 2010, Eliezer was awarded a certificate of appreciation by the board of the Recanati-Chase-Rashi Foundation, which gave an annual prize to a social worker for social entrepreneurship. On the certificate was written: "The evaluation committee found that you initiated and implemented praiseworthy work with the potential to lead to progress in the life of the individual and the community through the Israel Free Loan Association that enables interest-free loans to people of low income, and is worth bringing to the attention of social workers and managers in the welfare systems."

Prior to his 80th birthday, Eliezer decided to resign as chairman of Ogen. He asked Edward Cohen, a member of the association's board and chairman of its finance committee, to replace him. Cohen, who was himself nearing the age of 70, declined, but Eliezer didn't give up. Six months later he asked Cohen to reconsider, and Cohen again refused. The third time he used the name of Bob Gottesman, the association's biggest donor, who was friendly with Cohen. Eliezer told Edward that Gottesman insisted that Edward would replace him. This time Cohen agreed to consider the request and after consulting with his family agreed to take on the role for five years, until he reached the age of 75. He also decided to appoint two deputies from within the board in the hope of training one of them to succeed him. The two deputies were Ohad Eini, Eliezer's son-in-law, a real estate appraiser by profession, who today works as a government appraiser, and Adv. Ofir Ozeri, the son of Yechiel Ozeri, Eliezer and Rivka's old friend, who was also a member of the board for many years.

In September, 2011, Eliezer retired from his role as chairman of the association after twenty-one years and was appointed its president. As the president of the association, he continued to be active in it. Beyond his active membership on the board, Eliezer was diligent in continuing to arrive at the office, would speak with the employees and also with the clients who came to receive loans.

In his conversations with the loan applicants, Eliezer wanted to know their personal stories and hardships, in order to streamline the association's activities and adapt the responses to the changing needs of the applicants.

In 2012, Eliezer won the Knesset Speaker's Prize. The reasons the award committee gave were, among other things, the following: "Professor Jaffe founded the Israel Free Loan Association in 1990. When it comes to providing a loan, as opposed to a grant or [non-returnable] financial support, it is a process in which the borrower takes responsibility for his actions and financial future. This is a tremendous and wonderful endeavor. Up until now the association has given more than 40,000 loans, which are for 40,000 households in Israel, and has provided more than $130 million since its inception.

"Its operations and clients are spread throughout the country, and belong to all population groups. Professor Jaffe has been the chairman of the association since its establishment on a volunteer basis. While he was still in academia, the volunteering was close to his heart and he developed the subject of non-profit research, volunteering and philanthropy. He began his work in the field as one of the officials giving the loan, filling out the application forms, and he also managed the operation of the organization from the beginning until it reached its current dimensions. The association has become an address that fills the void created by the government which failed to address all social needs. Thanks to the character of Professor Jaffe

and the high credibility of the association and its employees and the responsible and transparent management of the funds, many philanthropists have chosen the association as a destination for their direct donations."

In the same year, Eliezer also received the Yakir Yerushalayim ("Worthy Citizen of Jerusalem") Decoration along with eleven other city residents. The committee's reasons read: "For the activity of Professor Eliezer Jaffe as a researcher and consultant for the well-being of the underprivileged, for volunteering for populations in distress in Jerusalem and for being an example and role model for dedication, he is awarded the decoration Yakir Yerushalayim."

In 2013, Eliezer turned 80. The members of Ogen wanted to hold a festive event in his honor but he did not want to. Only when he was told that the association would be at the center of the event and not him, did Eliezer agree. The event, which took place at the Menachem Begin Heritage Center in Jerusalem under the title "From Vision to Reality," was defined as a conference marking the 25th anniversary of the association's founding and on the occasion of its founder reaching his 80th birthday. During the conference, tribute was also paid to Yona Cohen, the director of the association who retired.

Eliezer's modesty, when it came to the association, was also reflected in his warm attitude toward its employees. Throughout the years, during his every visit to the association's offices, Eliezer made sure to stop by all the employees, ask how they were doing, talk to them and offer them coffee. Every staff meeting that Eliezer conducted opened with his thank you to the employees for their dedicated work. Eliezer repeatedly told the employees that the success of the association is credited to all the employees and the volunteers, and not to the credit of one person.

Every year, the association would hold a joint tour day for

employees and volunteers. It was important to Eliezer that these tours include visits to business owners who had received loans from the association, in order to illustrate to the employees and volunteers the association's great contribution to borrowers. Once it was a new jewelry store that received initial assistance from the association, another time a clothing store that had run into difficulties, and another time a carpentry shop that had needed support. The employees and volunteers were happy to see the fruits of their labor with their own eyes.

Eliezer also made sure to take care of the welfare of the association's employees. If he heard that the electric kettle or toaster used by the employees had broken down, the next day he would show up at the office with a new kettle or toaster. When the association was still on Azza Road, it was located on the second floor of a building with no elevator. One day Eliezer saw Nir Machluf, now the director of the association's finance department, climbing the stairs to the office with large, heavy cartons of paperwork. The next day, Eliezer arrived at the office with a small utility cart in his hand. Nir was happy with the cart and also moved by Eliezer's gesture and the fact that he had thought of it. His appreciation for Eliezer increased even more when he heard from whom Eliezer had bought the cart. Eliezer did not buy it in a store, but from a simple peddler in the Mea She'arim neighborhood who walked around selling various items for a living. "Eliezer was not satisfied with doing a kindness to me," says Nir. "He went to find someone else to whom he could also be kind. It's a small story but it symbolizes to me his perception of life, to help as many people as possible."

## Chapter Fifteen

## Farewell

In the last years of his life, Eliezer suffered from various medical problems, but he insisted on maintaining his regular routine as much as possible. His attitude to his medical condition was very practical and devoid of sentimentality or self-pity. He noted the appointments with his doctors in his diary as "meetings." Tom Eini, his grandson, tells the following story:

"During the army I was troubled by the condition of my knees that ached throughout the service, and eventually I had to have surgery. I shared my pain and my fears with Saba, who was an expert on pain, yet also the great victor who always managed to stay in good spirits. He advised me to simply, 'Take pills, there is no reason to suffer.' For him the body was a means to an end, and the investment in it should be sufficient to enable a person to perform the really important actions in life - doing good, giving, and investing in the family. "

Indeed, in addition to his continued involvement in the Israel Free Loan Association, Eliezer spent a lot of time with the family he loved so much. The grandchildren who grew up visited him often and had meaningful in-depth conversations with him, in which they got to know more about his worldview on various matters. Ido Eini, the son of Naomi and Ohad, says he had an ongoing discussion with

his grandfather about whichever public issue it would be worthwhile to act upon and influence. While Ido believed that it was better to work with strong groups of people who might change reality, Eliezer argued that one should work among weak populations that are on the margins of society. When Ido told him that in his yeshiva, in addition to Jewish studies, they also studied philosophy and economics, Eliezer asked him what he intended to do in the future with those studies. Ido replied that he would be happy to teach in institutions like the yeshiva where he studied. Eliezer looked his grandson in the eye and said that he should step out of his natural environment, and teach in other places that need this kind of content more.

On another occasion, Ido told his grandfather that he was planning to fly abroad for a few months. When Eliezer heard that Ido was planning to travel alone, he told him that every person must have at least one person to share his experiences with. "I had your grandmother," he said. "You must also find at least one partner to experience this trip with." On another occasion, when Ido talked to his grandfather about the world of education, Eliezer told him, "Every education, formal and informal, is meant first of all to educate yourself. If you have reached a point where you educated yourself and moved things forward in reality, then you are a good product of the educational system. "

Nadav Zimmerman, the son of Yael and Moshe, also talks about the push he received from his grandfather to engage in social action. "His message has always been that when you see something in reality that you can change, do it and act with all your might. Saba was very happy when I told him I wanted to work in areas like social work or psychology, where you work with people." Eliezer was happy when his grandchildren invited him to come and talk in their classrooms about his social enterprises. Even when it came to elementary school

children, he found a way to convey social messages to young children and to empower them. In a conversation with children in the second grade, the class of his grandson Noam Zimmerman, Eliezer told them about the establishment of the loan association and told the children that they too could do similar deeds. He asked them what they thought was missing in the classroom, and when one of the children replied that many children were losing *kippot* (yalmukes) and kippa clips, Eliezer responded enthusiastically and suggested to the children to set up a g'mach of kippot and clips. "Every one of you can do something," he told the children, and shortly afterwards he donated three kippot to the new g'mach.

The grandchildren were fortunate to experience the social sensitivity of their grandfather on various occasions. At one of the Shabbat dinners with Ruti and Udi Palmor, their daughter Hallel Palmor, who had recently enlisted in the army, shared fresh experiences with them from her basic training. Among other things, she told them about three female soldiers in her platoon who were granted exemption from prolonged standing and expressed her objection to it. The reaction of most of those sitting around the table was a cynical reaction to the female soldiers who were granted the exemption. Eliezer, on the other hand, told his granddaughter that the same female soldiers should be admired because, despite their physical difficulties, they nevertheless enlisted in the army.

Tom Eini relates that during one of his visits to his grandfather he brought with him a member of the hesder yeshiva [in which he studied] who immigrated to Israel from the United States and was experiencing difficulties in getting acclimated. "Saba took an interest in everyone and I knew that my friend would find a willing ear, and would be helped by him, and so it was. Saba spoke to him at length and was genuinely interested in him."

Renana Palmor says she invited her grandfather to the graduation event of a painting class she attended for several years. The class teacher spoke at the end of the event and invited the guests to ask questions. Eliezer asked the teacher how she succeeded in maintaining her excitement through the years from the paintings made by the children in the class. The teacher was very moved by Eliezer's question. Later she told Renana that this was the first time at events of this kind that she was asked about her feelings.

It was very important to Eliezer that his grandchildren receive an academic education. He did not try to direct them to certain professions but it was important to him that they achieve a high professional level in whichever field they chose to pursue.

Roi Jaffe, the son of Uri and Keren, recalled a conversation he had with his grandfather one Shabbat, when he was 15. Eliezer asked Roi what he would like to do when he grows up, and what he would like to study at university. Roi replied, "My dream is to be a bus driver." Eliezer looked into Roi's eyes with a serious look and told him, "I have no problem with you being a bus driver but do not give up the opportunity to acquire an academic education."

Later, after graduating high school and serving in the army, Roi decided to study accounting. Roi says that he once asked his grandfather if his academic "pedigree" [as Eliezer's grandson] could help him during his studies. "Saba told me: 'I believe in you Roi, and if you want to achieve something, you can achieve it on your own, without shortcuts.' Saba was a very honest person and did not believe in 'protektzia' [playing favorites] of any kind."

The importance that Eliezer and Rivka saw in higher education was realized in the opening of dedicated savings funds for higher education for all their grandchildren. The grandchildren and family members can still quote Eliezer's statement today: "Never disqualify

yourself from applying or trying anything you are interested in."

Along with meaningful conversations, Eliezer also really enjoyed having fun with his grandchildren. He went with them to movies, plays, lectures and performances, and sometimes just sat with them watching TV, with a bowl of popcorn. When they would see a tightrope walker on TV, or another stuntman performing a dangerous act, Eliezer would say to his grandchildren: "It's easy! I could have done that too!" He particularly loved Bugs Bunny, who earned the nickname "Bugs." Cartoons starring Bugs are known almost by heart by his grandchildren.

Gitit Zimmerman says that her grandfather invited her to a scientific lecture for the university's retirees and she dropped the average age there dramatically. Another time she went with Eliezer to a performance of a vocal band from the USA.

Eliezer received many visits from his grandchildren. When they came to see him, he would ask them to make him an omelet or pancakes, and he would shower exaggerated praise on their culinary skills. Hadar Jaffe (Rosen) says: "My family and close friends know that I am not known as a great cook and when people come to me for a meal, everything is bought and served in good taste. And I take comfort in the fact that, for one person only, my grandfather, I was a superb cook, a culinary expert and chef on the highest possible level. Saba Eli loved everything I prepared, whether it was a burnt omelet with ketchup, or cornflakes that I gave him in a large bowl full of milk, or a pampering and decadent pancake smothered in maple syrup. I would prepare a plate and arrange vegetables and fruit in the form of flowers, a smiley or the sun, and enjoy seeing Saba relishing every bite."

Eliezer also occasionally invited his adult grandchildren to restaurants, where they used to sit, talk, listen and strengthen the bond

between them, the grandchildren admiring a grandfather who easily connects to the younger-adult generation out of genuine interest.

Hadar Palmor tells of a grandfather who also collaborated with his grandchildren's unconventional initiatives. "When I was 16, I had the idea of having my birthday party on the roof of Saba's building. I asked Saba if he agreed and he immediately said 'Happily!' and gave me money to duplicate the key to the roof. One of my friends took it upon herself to organize the event, and on the day of the party, when my mother called, she heard the same friend giving orders to Saba, as she was dangling rows of lights from the roof, down to the porch of his apartment, and he was going along with it happily...It was only one more example of his youthful spirit."

The children of the Zimmerman family tell of the affection that Saba Eliezer had for their dog, Puma. In order for the dog to not gain too much weight, the family members tried not to feed her large amounts of food. Eliezer, in his great affection for the dog, broke the family rules and he used to throw her food, especially cakes and sweets, under the Shabbat table.

Tom Eini tells of his grandfather's bet with his grandson Assaf (Zimmerman) regarding the question: Which of Uri's children will marry first, Roi or Hadar. "Saba bet on Roi, and Asaf on Hadar. The terms of the bet were that the winner must bring the loser Saba's favorite cake - lemon pie. It was clear to everyone that no matter who won, Saba would eat that pie..."

Eliezer expressed his young spirit not only among the family. One day he got the urge to drive up to Mount Hermon, in the Golan Heights. On the way, he picked up a number of young hitchhikers who also wanted to get to Mount Hermon, and even surprised them by pampering them with cable car tickets. When one of his children called him, Eliezer reported that he was on Mount Hermon, sitting

around a gas burner having coffee along with the young hitchhikers he had picked up along the way. Even in his last years, when he used a cane, he did not give up hiking. He would toss the cane with a sharp motion into the back of the car, and set off. He used to hide chocolates in the glove compartment for "emergencies."

Eliezer's other hobby was fishing and his son Uri joined him many times. Sometimes, when he brought Eliezer to his home for Shabbat, Uri took the opportunity to stop on the way with his father and fish.

Despite his physical limitations, Eliezer traveled to visit his grandchildren in their schools and attended their military graduation ceremonies. He even cooperated in wearing a humorous shirt that one of the families had prepared for their son in preparation for the graduation ceremony of his officers' course.

Tom Eini, his grandson, recounts: "One day while I was sitting with Saba in the kitchen, we talked a little bit about politics. I remember Saba analyzing that the motive behind many of President Obama's activities was the president's need to be loved. This kind of analysis – looking at the situation from the human, psychological perspective of the leader – was new to me and gave me a significant tool for analyzing events. For Saba, the importance of the human-emotional factor in decision-making was crucial."

Another memory of Tom's was connected to his first year at the yeshiva, when he spent more and more time with his grandfather: "One day Saba invited me to join him at an opera to which he had received two free VIP tickets. I happily joined him. The opera – 'L'elisir D'amore' ('The Elixir of Love') – was performed at Sultan's Pool, under the stars, and was very nice. It was a little cool. Each VIP guest received a bag with all kinds of 'swag,' including a small blanket. During the performance Saba saw that a young woman sitting near us was trembling from the cold, and he gave her his blanket.

I, of course, wanted to give him my blanket, but he refused. At the end of the performance the young man and woman sitting near us disappeared with Saba's blanket. It bothered him, not because it indicated ungratefulness on their part, but because of their basic lack of caring, their lack of basic human ethics – 'You received something on loan, return it.'"

In 2016, Edward Cohen reached the age of 75 and asked to retire as chairman of the association. The person who replaced Cohen in his position was Ofir Ozeri, a member of the board who until then had served as one of the chairman's two deputies, alongside Ohad Eini. Shortly after Ozeri took office, Joe Rosen, the association's CEO, retired, and the association's management set up a search committee to look for a new CEO. One of the prominent candidates was Sagi Balasha, who had returned a year earlier from the United States, where he had directed IAC, an organization of the Israeli community in the United States, for four years. The members of the search committee were very impressed with Balasha, but he made it clear to them that he would join the association only if he was allowed to make significant changes. Balasha, who was very impressed by the association's activities, claimed that as an organization rolling over two hundred million shekels received from donors, the association should step up, leverage its money, and become a social bank that will also provide subsidized interest loans to business owners and customers who cannot receive credit from banks.

The members of the search committee debated the issues and finally asked Balasha to meet with members of the association's board, including Eliezer. Balasha presented them with his doctrine regarding the future of the association and won the enthusiastic support of Eliezer. Today, Balasha says that without Eliezer's support for the revolutionary ideas he proposed at the time, he would have had great

difficulty convincing the other members of the board. "Although he was the founder and the oldest person on the board, Eliezer was the most open, the most creative, the most attentive and the most liberating. It is customary to expect someone who has established something meaningful, to cling to the past and resist change, but Eliezer, with keen thoughtfulness and wisdom, understood the present and envisioned the future."

On September 1, 2016, Balasha took over as CEO of the Israel Free Loan Association. On the first day of his job, he met with Eliezer and talked to him about the future of the association. Balasha asked questions and recorded Eliezer's answers. "We built a beautiful machine here but it's not utilized enough," said Eliezer. "There's a lot of money out there, a lot more can be done and I would like to help more people. We need to be relevant to the plight and needs of Israeli society today, to examine new avenues and see if our organization is suitable for them." Balasha asked Eliezer if he would agree to cooperate with other associations and Eliezer said he would be happy to do so, but it was important to him that such a relationship would not cause the organization to stop its activities of saving people from financial collapse. Balasha asked about the possibility of cooperating with government ventures and Eliezer said that the association had previously tried to do so, but had not succeeded thus far.

Then Balasha asked Eliezer if he had any objection to rebranding the organization and even to changing its name. "I have no objection to rebranding and to a name change if it will help us gain more donors and connections," said Eliezer, "but in every new constellation one must retain the mechanism that will continue to give interest-free loans."

During his first week in office, Balasha met not only with Eliezer but also with Bob Gottesman, the association's major donor.

Gottesman also conveyed to Balasha an expectation of increasing the scope of the association's actions and expressed a desire to hear about new moves that would expand it. Balasha presented Gottesman with his new plans and Gottesman responded enthusiastically.

He called Eliezer and promised to give the association fifteen million dollars to carry out the new moves. Eliezer felt that momentum had been created for change. In January, 2017, Gottesman arrived in Israel, and met with Eliezer and with the association's board members. The meeting took place at Eliezer's home due to his deteriorating medical condition.

"Eliezer pushed to make the moves as quickly as possible," said Balasha. "He wanted to know that the plans were put into action. There was a feeling that Eliezer sensed that perhaps this was his last meeting with Gottesman and therefore he needed to get the most out of it."

A month later, the board held a meeting on the future of the association and the possibility of turning it into a social bank. Balasha says that Eliezer was very dominant at that meeting and expressed support for the association to start granting, in addition to interest-free loans to business owners, subsidized loans. As will be explained below, the interest was intended only to cover the operating costs of deposits, and not for profit. The chairman of the board, Ofir Ozeri, also supported the move.

During the nine months that passed from the time that Balasha took office and until Eliezer's death, quite a few changes were made to the association, all with Eliezer's consent and encouragement. One of the changes was the opening of the association's loans to all Israeli society, including the Arab sector. For more than twenty years, the association has provided loans only to Jews. Eliezer's decision that the association would focus on Jewish society had stemmed from

the fact that the Torah prohibition on taking interest applies only to Jews. Balasha managed to persuade Eliezer to change his position.

"He understood that if the association wanted to establish a social bank and be a state institution that receives support from the state, it could not be sectoral," said Balasha. Another change was the establishment of a fund for high-risk borrowers designed to provide a guarantee to borrowers in a difficult financial situation who were unable to find guarantors to obtain a loan. The loan to such borrowers was conditioned on them undergoing a [financial] rehabilitation program.

Another new area for the association was assisting young couples in purchasing apartments. In March, 2017, the association connected to the "Achim L'Bayit" ("Brothers for a Home" in English) organization, which provides financial education to young families on their way to purchasing their first apartment. The joint program created by the association with Achim L'Bayit is called "Ogen L'Bayit" ("Anchor for the Home" in English). It combines professional guidance, education and coaching by Achim L'Bayit together with the financial assistance of the association. Achim L'Bayit brought to the program its extensive experience in working with families, and the association brought the possibility of providing interest-free loans. Ogen L'Bayit offers young families a loan of up to one hundred thousand shekels without interest, to complete the equity required to purchase the apartment. Parallel with these moves, collaborations were also established with government ventures. The Ogen L'Bayit program operated a joint project with the Prime Minister's Office and the Ministry of Housing, in whose framework it accompanied about 200 families from Ethiopia in the purchasing of an apartment.

But the jewel in the crown of the changes was undoubtedly the preparations to make the association the first social bank in Israel.

Since its inception, for more than twenty-five years, the association has only received donations for interest-free loan purposes and had not held deposits. The association's first step on its way to becoming a social bank was the establishment of an impact fund in which deposits from social investors would be invested. The idea was that social investors would invest in the Impact Fund an amount of at least one million dollars as long-term investment. The investments would enable the Impact Fund to use the money to provide large and significant loans. The plan was for the association to collect very low interest from those who borrowed from this fund, and that interest would be used to cover the cost of operating the fund and the non-repaid loans. At the end of the investment period the entire amount would be returned to investors with interest of up to one percent.

The association set itself the primary goal of raising NIS 100 million for the Impact Fund from strategic investors, including private investors, corporations and philanthropists. Within a few months, about sixty million shekels were recruited. In the next phase, the association planned to offer banking services such as current account management, investment portfolio management and credit card issuance - activities from which it was also expected to benefit. These services were expected to attract stronger clients who would ensure that in spite of the fact that the main target audience were those of the weaker population, the new social bank would be stable. The ultimate goal of the social bank was to give banking services at affordable rates even to those who suffered from limited access to traditional banking and credit services.

At the end of April, 2017, a few weeks before Eliezer's death, Ofir Ozeri and Sagi Balasha arrived at Eliezer's home to examine with him the possibility of changing the name of the association as part

of its renewal and expansion process. The two were very impressed by Eliezer's openness to changing the name of the association and the rebranding. The new name, chosen by the board, was "Ogen" – "Anchor" in English.

The members of the association conducted videotaped interviews with Eliezer in the last months of his life. In these interviews, Eliezer talked about his social enterprises, his research and of course about Ogen. In his words, he wanted to convey a message to young people: That they should take responsibility in the social field and take the lead in moving things forward. "I tell people who are thinking about aliya, and young Israelis, that there is still a lot of pioneering waiting for them. A lot depends on them and the challenges are not over. Every day is a challenge. Every time an issue arises that you feel you can be involved in, and in which you can help and change something for the better – it is absolutely possible. If there is a subject that comes up and you feel that you have a hand in that issue, or an opinion, you need to do what you can, to make an impact. I believe that one man in the right place with the right idea and the right tools, can change a lot of things, and you do not know who the man is. I always say this to my students. 'Two or three of the forty in the class can be leaders.'"

In the last year of his life, Eliezer's medical condition worsened. He occasionally used an oxygen balloon to breathe, and an electric scooter to get around. Despite the new restrictions, Eliezer tried to remain as active as possible. Sometimes his children had to insist that he take the oxygen balloon with him to his activities at the association or to the synagogue. Eliezer also did not lose his legendary optimism, did not complain about his pain, and maintained a good mood. On the day he was defined as a patient no longer independent, in need of intensive nursing, he insisted on going alone to a

movie at the cinema while demonstrating the triumph of the mind over the body.

In time, Eliezer was forced to visit the hospital frequently, and even to be hospitalized for extended periods. The children, their spouses and his many grandchildren surrounded him with love throughout that period and arranged their schedules so they could be by his side around the clock on the days he was hospitalized. One day Eliezer said to his daughter Yael, "I'm lucky you're here with me all the time, helping me, consulting the doctors, filling out forms and taking care of everything. But what do people do who have no family or help from friends? Maybe you should find out if there are associations that help in that area, and if there are not any, maybe you should create such an organization, that will help the sick who have no family."

Yael was amazed that even in his critical medical condition, her father was thinking about the needs of other patients, and of ideas to help them. When doctors entered his room as part of daily doctor visits, Eliezer said: "I want you to know that I really appreciate you coming to my humble room ... you are so nice and work hard and do not get enough appreciation." In an honest and direct conversation with doctors, he turned them into private individuals, and himself into "Eliezer."

One of the treatments that Eliezer had to undergo in those days was having fluids pumped from the lungs to ease [pressure on] the respiratory system. The treatment was performed with Eliezer sitting on his bed while a doctor inserted a long needle into his back to pump the fluid from the lungs. Eliezer was bothered by the fact that he could not see the face of the doctor performing the treatment. In one of the treatments, after the needle was removed from his back, he asked the doctor to turn to him so that he could see his face. "I

want to see the face of the one who is helping me to breathe," he explained. The doctor sat down opposite Eliezer and Eliezer began asking him personal questions about his area of expertise and praising him for the way he performed the treatment. "You did it gently and you did not hurt me," he told the doctor. "Thanks to you I can breathe better now. It's important for me to thank you personally for this treatment."

One day Eliezer's little granddaughter, Shahar Eini, came to visit him. She approached him and asked: "Saba, do you want something? May I help you?" Eliezer did not need anything but wanted to give his little granddaughter a sense that she too could help, so he answered her, "I want to lift the back of the bed a little, so that I may be more comfortable. Do you think that you can understand how to do that?" Shahar spent about a quarter of an hour activating the bed's adjustable mechanism, pressing wherever possible, raising and lowering the bed, with her grandfather directing her and thanking her for her significant contribution...

Ido Eini relates a conversation he had with his grandfather, in those days, about death. He read him a poem by the poet Heinrich Heine relating to death and asked him if he thought about it. Eliezer, who did not shy away from the question, said to his grandson, "I do not understand why when I am here in the hospital you talk to me about death. I do not think about death but about life. There is no reason to think about death during life. If you think about death during life, you're already considered as dead." When his children asked him what he wanted them to write on his headstone, he replied, "Whatever you want, but do not exaggerate." Even on difficult days, Eliezer kept his sense of humor.

When he needed a chest X-ray, he asked the technician if he should smile to make the X-ray look more beautiful. One day his

grandson, Dvir Palmor, came to visit him and Dvir asked Eliezer to test him on his command of English words in preparation for a test. Eliezer read the list of words out loud, but at one point, Dvir noticed that the list was going longer than what was expected. He soon discovered that his grandfather had added his own words to the list, praising him for his knowledge...

And there were also moments of black humor. One day, when Eliezer had many visitors, his daughter Ruti said to him in admiration, "Look how many people come to visit you. You are so important to everyone." Eliezer looked at her and replied with a half-smile, "I am preparing you for the days of the shiva..."

Dr. Neta Goldschmidt was Eliezer's doctor in the last months of his life. She says that Eliezer was very sober and well aware of his medical condition and at one point even knew that his days were numbered. "He had a certain sadness about him, but not depression or anger that usually exist with patients at this stage. In my opinion, he skipped the stages of anger and depression, although he may have experienced them but did not project it." Goldschmidt says that Eliezer focused on knowing the medical facts and even when he was aware of the severity of his condition, he maintained high morale. "Even during the last stages, he always looked forward, expressed acceptance of the situation, saw the good things, and rejoiced in all that he was privileged to have had in his lifetime. He was fully committed to the struggle for his life, but out of knowledge and recognition that he was not sure he would succeed and out of acceptance. It was very impressive." One day Eliezer told his children, "I think I made good choices in life. I would not change most of the things I did."

Even during his illness, Eliezer continued to be interested in all the people he met. In the last weeks of his life, Eliezer was assisted by an ambulance company that transported him three times a week for

dialysis at the hospital. The ambulance crew was mostly made up of ultra-Orthodox. Eliezer, as was his custom, used to interview them on the way to the hospital. He asked them what they were studying, and advised them to study core subjects (English, Mathematics and Hebrew Language) and then proceed to degree studies. He inquired about the ambulance company, asked if they would like to expand and gave them the phone numbers of Ogen so they could purchase another ambulance.

In mid-May, 2017, Eliezer was told that he had won the "Bonei Zion" ("Builders of Zion") Prize of the Nefesh B'Nefesh organization for that year. The award is given annually to selected immigrants from English-speaking countries who have made a significant contribution to the State of Israel. The award committee chose to award it to Eliezer for his contribution in the field of welfare, philanthropy and the third sector in Israel. The prize ceremony was scheduled for mid-June, but Eliezer did not merit to receive his award. He also did not attend his granddaughter Chen Jaffe's wedding scheduled for early June. At noon on Thursday, May 25, 2017, the 29th of Iyar, 5777, at the age of 83, he returned his soul to its Creator.

Deep mourning fell upon Eliezer's family and on the many who loved him. The obituary issued by the association read: "Professor Jaffe left behind four children, grandchildren, great-grandchildren, and tens of thousands of Israeli families who prospered thanks to the charitable endeavors he established."

On Friday, Rosh Chodesh Sivan, many came to Har HaMenuchot in Jerusalem to accompany Eliezer on his final journey. His eldest son Uri said in his eulogy: "Thank you Abba for years of learning. You gave us all a lesson on how to be good people, giving people and how to always think of others. Thank you for good 'tips' for life such as: 'Marriage is a serious thing,' 'Believe in something and go with it

to the end,' 'Honesty in life is everything,' 'Flowers for Shabbat - do not forget!'" Uri thanked all those who attended the funeral and said to them, "Abba would probably say now, 'Friends, there is work to do, tasks to accomplish. Continue with your lives.'"

Yael talked in her eulogy about her father's love for all people and his boundless giving to others. "You knew how to say thank you for everything to everyone. When we would come to you for Shabbat and bring food you would say, 'You know, I appreciate it so much. You are doing a great mitzva. You know how much I love you and how proud I am of you.'"

Naomi also spoke in her eulogy about the place and time Eliezer was taken. "Today is Friday and you are buried in the land of Jerusalem. 'Yedid nefesh sheli, Av Harahaman…'[22] Friend of my soul, merciful Father, there was a spirit that carried your body and helped you reach the synagogue without oxygen to stand in prayer. You say farewell to us between Jerusalem Day and the Feast of the Giving of the Torah (Shavuot), a religious Zionist combination of holiness and holiness. Your life was a life of kindness and faith, returning great interest to the world and leaving it flawless and pure."

Ruti spoke about the life of wholeness her father had been privileged to live. "Being in your company, Abba, was like being in the company of a great engine that constantly pushes for meaningful action, and yet knows how to refill its batteries and enjoy life. You were the most serious and the funniest. A man of vision and of

---

22  A reference to the Shabbat song, "Yedid Nefesh," which begins, "Yedid nefesh, Av Harahaman…' usually attributed to Rabbi Elazar Azikri who lived in Safed in the 16th century. Naomi's intentional play on words was connecting the song, written to God, with her feelings for her father.